The Pheasant Hunter's
Action Adventure Cookbook

Explore a collection of recipes, tall tales, and expert tips-from puppy training to perfecting a wine reduction sauce. Master field dressing and butchering with innovative techniques that honor tradition and science, prioritize cleanliness, and elevate flavor and simplicity.

By Richard Moran

This book: 27,800 words. 50 photos or illustrations. 3 chapters about butchering, 9 main recipe classes, 6 side dishes, 7 short stories, and more.

Dedication

My spectacular wife Felicia insisted I get a dog then patiently endured the consequences. She puts up with a lot of nonsense.

Acknowledgments

This book would not have been possible without help from my friends at Scribophile, especially Karl Van Lear, Jena Rodas, and Monty Burr for their invaluable editing and advice. Thanks to Andy for taking me on several preserve hunts, and the Wisconsin Department of Natural Resources and Pheasants Forever for their efforts in stocking wild lands and habitat preservation.

Without the talented, photogenic and all-around good dog, there would be no book.

Legal Stuff

Chapter 0. Introduction

I remember when my Labrador dropped our first pheasant at my feet. It was about 5 years ago, and I wasn't sure what to do. Fifty pheasants later, I'm ready to explain.

In this book, you will learn how to turn a bird into mouthwatering, ready-to-cook meat using hygienic, easy, and efficient methods. Hunters often turn their nose up at pheasant legs because they have forgotten age-old techniques of butchering and cooking. Learn how to enjoy the whole bird. Your taste-buds will thank you.

Everything I present is simple and easy to follow, even for novice cooks and hunters.

Grill, bread and fry, or poach the delicate, flavorful breasts. Slow cook succulent thighs and drumsticks in tomato or wine sauces. Make soup from the carcass and giblets. Each element will be cooked to perfection, tailored to their individual requirements. Recipes are organized into main dishes and side dishes with beverage suggestions. You can make special meals to celebrate your catch, no matter which cut of meat or cooking method you choose. There are recipes for leftovers and for stretching a bird for extra guests.

Plucking a pheasant is laborious and time-consuming. The process begs the bird to be roasted. But the breast meat is best cooked in six minutes while the legs take hours. The solution is simple. Don't pluck pheasants.

I've salted seven short stories among the butchering and cooking bits to provide action, instruction, and amusement. Come along on my pheasant hunting trips where I survive everything from training a puppy to ninja rabbit attacks. Action, adventure, and a cookbook!

Chapter 1. The Chicken Wagon

I rolled in a field of thorns after jumping from a speeding car? No, my Labrador puppy was teething. He had torn my face and hands bloody for the past month.

Needle sharp baby teeth pushed painfully through his gums. He'd gnaw everything he could reach for relief, stimulation, or to play with me, his littermate. I yipped every time his attention wandered from his chew toy to my hand. Sleepy puppy would wag his tail, crawl up my chest like an angel, then bite my face. Lab puppies have a demonic phase.

Sure, he'd receive a time-out in his crate for chomps. But no suggestion from books or the internet could curb the mayhem. I would yip and cry like a hurt puppy, tell him 'no', deny him attention. He would stop immediately, pulling away, his mouth of little daggers gouging bloody scratches across my skin. Then he'd roll over, tail wagging and ears perked, the picture of innocence. He meant no harm.

I took his name, "Havoc", from Antony's line in Shakespeare's Julius Caesar, "Cry Havoc, let slip the dogs of war." No war dog, he was a roly-poly, playful little Labrador pup. But he was making me cry. Offsetting the teething damage, he had been instantly house trained.

There was only one accident, and it was my fault. Wagging his tail, jumping at the door to go outside, I let him out of his crate, but fumbled too long with cream for my coffee. Puppy pee leaked. When a puppy needs to go, he needs to go now.

He was learning to sit and target. "Target" meant "come over here and boop your nose on my palm." That command led to many others. He learned to untangle his leash if he walked on the wrong side of a signpost, following my target hand to unwrap. He learned commands to get into his crate, get in the car, and to lie on his place on the rug. All using the target command.

I created a new trick called "give me a kiss". I would toss him a biscuit for a nose-boop 'target' on my cheek. A nip earned five minutes in the crate. My face healed, and he became quite skillful at catching treats in mid-air.

Around six months, Havoc's bright white, comfortable adult teeth had filled in. My face was no longer mincemeat. Biting people was unthinkable. He was gentle with puppies, babies, and kids but still roughhoused with the big dogs. And he became ball-crazy.

Havoc showed a talent for catching his ball on the bounce. He'd leap high in the air to grab it. If I threw the ball less than twenty yards, he'd often catch it over his shoulder. Labrador, ball, fetch. Like feet, socks and shoes, it's a natural combination. We were playing off-leash, in an eighty-acre fenced dog park.

He knew his recall command, but all bets were off if he found other dogs to play with. Anyone with a dog could complete my shouted command of "come!" He would run over to the nearest human, wagging his tail, job done. This irritating misconception lasted a few months.

We began walking in public wildlife hunting areas, off-leash. He was too young to hunt, but when we heard gunfire in the distance, he got a reward. That sound was associated with fun and treats. Then we came across pheasant tail feathers on the trail.

That was a big deal. "This is the Bird. Bird." Havoc smelled the feathers and got more snacks. One day, he found a ring-neck carcass from a hawk kill.

"Good dog! You found the bird!" Biscuits and praise showered the happy retriever. Next pheasant season, we went hunting for real.

One pocket of my field jacket had dog biscuits, the other had shotgun shells. When the dog found feathers or a pheasant carcass, I doled out lavish praise and treats. He got them for searching patterns within 20 yards. It didn't make a difference that the rewards weren't foo-foo bacon snacks with fake cheese. He loved doing the job he was bred for.

Between the dog's nose and my eyes, we learned where the birds were not. Eventually, luck favored the persistent. Havoc flushed a bird. A beautiful golden bird with a green neck and red head. Its wing beat was explosive and clucks filled the air.

I missed. I missed with three booming shots. My hands trembled and shoulder ached from where I mounted the butt improperly in haste.

The dog chased the unharmed bird beyond a hedge. I called. He returned promptly, at a gallop, ears flapping as he hurdled through the marsh grass. Treats. Some people call positive reinforcement bribery, but I call it payment. After establishing a behavior, random payments.

Havoc flushed pheasants a half a dozen times over the next few weeks, but they escaped my shots. He was enjoying this game more than I was. But then, by luck or skill, I shot one.

Its wings folded and down it went, out of sight beyond a thick honeysuckle grove. Havoc came bounding back through the marsh, bird in mouth, and dropped it at my feet. Praise rained down. I was proud of my dog, and he strutted all day, tail up and ears perked. He had gotten his bird and brought it back.

The next summer, the patterning board at the club showed that my shotgun stock was too long. The excess length caused me to shoot to the left and explained my bruised upper arm. I cut off half an inch of wood and took a few trips to the skeet range. Much better.

Havoc was an enthusiastic upland bird dog. We found pheasants with better success the next fall, but the pup would hunt too far out. Birds he flushed were out of range.

Constantly calling him back with three soft whistles, I gave treats. Or I turned to walk away so he would have to dash back. After an hour and a half of this, fatigue kept him closer. He was a good bird dog when tired, but wearing him out wore my patience thin.

eBay saved the day. I bought a cheap thirty-dollar PetTrainer™ electronic collar. It could beep, vibrate with a buzz, or shock Havoc with a push of a button.

The buzz vibration was a tap on his shoulder. "Hey buddy, pay attention!" I would whistle softly three times. If he ignored me, buzz-buzzz-buzz. "Pay attention!" He learned to hunt within a twenty-five yard radius, courtesy of those buzzes and biscuits. He was learning.

His worst habit was chasing after the two sounds he loved most in the whole world: gunshots or pheasant cackles. When he heard those, he'd be gone for five minutes, enjoying his own little hunt while I called his name in frustration. My annoyance increased with every minute and every instance. Worse than bad manners, it wasn't safe. It was time to use the button that caused an electric shock.

Boom! He heard a shot and off he ran.

"Havoc!" I called. He was running away. "Buzz buzz buzz!" He was still running, ignoring me.

"SHOCK!"

He jumped in the air and made a pitiful yip, but he came running back. Praised and soothed for returning, I gave pats on the side and treats. He didn't know it was me, but I felt sorry for the pain I inflicted. Havoc learned after two repetitions. Well, three. He looked back at me with a guilty expression, giving it one last try before starting towards another gunshot. He was testing his hypothesis and got a zap. Bad habits in the field and at the dog park ended.

There are two differences between my $30 cheap collar and a nicer $600 unit. The charging port of our cheap radio receiver leaked, and you can't keep a Labrador out of the creek. So I wrapped five inches of black electrical tape around the module. The other difference is $570.

He loved putting his E-collar on; it meant adventure. Even if he no longer needed it.

My dog had grown from a little scamp puppy into a serious Upland Labrador. We found many more pheasants. This brings us around to the Chicken Wagon.

In south-central Wisconsin, our birds are raised in pens and then released to wander on public lands for hunting. Old-timers remember when the wild population was self-sustaining, but no longer.

Changes in agriculture, pesticides, over-hunting, and niche pressure from turkeys are blamed. So are predators like hawks, coyotes, and egg thieves like skunks and raccoons. Lost habitat is the critical factor.

The Department of Natural Resources and Pheasants Forever release adult birds while they work to correct the situation. Few will survive and reproduce, but someday they will. That's the goal.

Income from hunting licenses and a federal tax on ammunition pays the bill for habitat restoration, birds, and public hunting land. With none of these facts in mind, the dog and I were walking down a muddy fire-break trail on a fine weekday afternoon. I spotted tire tracks from a truck. The sign half-a-mile back said "No Vehicles Beyond This Point."

These tracks circled in a large meadow nestled in mixed forest. Large green pines to one side, bare oak and aspen at the other. The dog's tail wagged frantically as he nosed the grassland. Five pheasants cackled in unison as the whole covey* (see footnote) exploded airborne. I raised my gun. Boom! The dog brought a beautiful ring-neck back. We set off to find another. Five minutes later, the dog flushed a bevy of three more birds. I brought one down on the third shot. We set off towards home with two pretty pheasants in the back pocket of my jacket, our daily limit filled.

On our way back, we met a grizzled hunter with his friendly German Short-hair Pointer.

"Any luck?" he asked, as the dogs wagged tails and sniffed butts.

"Yes! There are lots of birds back there. I got a brace." I patted the side of my jacket. Long brown-and-white striped tail feathers stuck out from the rear game bag pocket.

The gentleman smiled at my enthusiasm. He pointed to the tire tracks. "Yep, that's the Chicken Wagon."

I tilted my head. "Chicken Wagon?"

"That's what we call a Department of Natural Resources stocking truck," he explained. "I hunt here often. Soon, you'll learn their schedules and routes, too. Keep it secret. A fella should earn that knowledge."

"Thanks for the tip!" I tapped my nose with my finger and we parted ways. For the rest of our second season, our hunting was based on crops, weather, and terrain. But we also scoured the trails for chicken wagon tracks and learned its habits and schedule. This led to several misadventures.

—

One warm October day, the dog and I were wading through four-foot-tall grass with ankle-twisting hummocks in the middle of a large marsh. This was pointer territory, but we had taken a shortcut.

I noticed a truck in the distance, driving from a gap in the woods.

"Chicken Wagon," I told the dog. "If we work that direction, maybe we'll have some luck."

The truck stopped in the distance. A man got out. I waved my orange cap at him, but he didn't seem to notice. Instead, he threw about eight pheasants into the marsh. Some flew short, some flew long. The dog got excited, his tail flagged madly.

"Well, this sort of spoils the illusion of hunting," I complained.

The Chicken Wagon proceeded along the perimeter of our marsh. It stopped again. The man got out.

"What the heck?" I asked the dog.

The man opened his truck and threw another dozen pheasants. They cackled and fluttered, flying every which way. Four of them flew right at us. I put the excited dog on his leash. The man got back in his truck and drove to the gate at the edge of the marsh.

"We'll wait for him to leave before shooting. That seems polite, right?"

But the man stopped again. He threw another dozen birds aloft. One flew over our heads. Some flapped into a privately owned cornfield, and some refused to fly at all. He had to shoo birds away from the front of the truck.

"This is no fun," I told the dog. I let him off his leash. "Let's get a bird and go home."

The dog went nuts, nose overloaded. The whole sixty acres must have smelled like bird, with pheasants running around like turbocharged chickens. We pushed through the long grass.

A pheasant startled me, it flushed right at my feet and flew straight away. Boom. I was stunned to see I had missed the easy shot. I shot and missed again. My third shot was wide, too. Missing these classic rising pheasant shots destroyed my confidence.

We walked back, and another bird flushed. I missed another three easy shots. The dog chased the flying bird, which kicked up two more. I scored another three misses. The dog flew through the marsh like a fox-red rocket, flushing birds hundreds of yards away, out of control, he stirred things up.

I had one shell left and felt like an idiot.

"Screw this." I unloaded the last shell into my hand. The dog was nearly out of sight, still making birds fly. I called. He came back, tongue lolling, panting heavily but overjoyed by the chase. He was the only one. My ears were red with shame.

We kicked up three more birds as we walked back to the car. All I fired at them were insults and the dog, confined by his leash, only gave a half-hearted tug.

I had mastered my temper by the time we reached our car. This encounter with the Chicken Wagon hadn't been fun. It ruined the day. We had been standing in a vast field while someone threw pheasants at us. There was no skill or exploration, no learning or merit to it. But we had done a good job scattering those birds about the marsh, the cornfield, the woods to the north and east and along the creek.

I drove home and reflected. The dog crashed in the back hatch, worn out. The next afternoon, we went back. Rather than enter the open marsh, we struggled into the rugged creek bed and its tangles. This was our preferred turf. A few birds must have hidden back there. The dog's nose didn't get overloaded, so he flushed a couple of birds, and I took each down with difficult crossing shots. Two birds, three shells. Confidence restored, I vowed to practice next summer at the trap field.

I told the dog if we came across the Chicken Wagon again, we'd scatter the birds and move on. The dog just tilted his head. I realized we were not beginners anymore.

Later in the season we set out on a crisp November Saturday. It was a week before Thanksgiving. Every parking area we scouted held at least three pickup trucks. We pulled into a remote lot with just one car.

I saw a man trudging towards us as I put on my jacket. I waved my hat, and he waved back. He had an obese black Labrador waddling ahead of him. I let my fit young dog out of the car, and that's when the man started shooting. Boom! Boom! Boom! Boom! Firing in an arc, dirt, leaves and old straw flew in the air. About 50 yards from the car, he was shooting at the ground. What was he doing? He was reloading.

His dog waddled around the field in front of him. Havoc was safe. I was about to dive for cover, then noticed the field was full of pheasants, all running around on the ground. Boom! Boom! Boom! The man fired in a direction away from us. Now I was worried about the safety of his fat dog.

It's unsportsmanlike to shoot at ground birds, and worse, so close to the parking lot. I didn't condone his action, but understood. He might be old, but he was acting like a beginner. It was a few days before Thanksgiving, so I hoped the old man had gotten a bird or two, that his wife would be pleased, and his dog enjoyed the exercise.

Doing my best to keep this generous holiday attitude, I whistled up my Lab and walked the other way. Havoc dashed to the left, cut sharply to the right and immediately flushed a pheasant. He leapt five feet into the air and grabbed the bird neatly around the body. Then he raced back, the flapping bird held firmly in his mouth. The bird's neck wrung, I stowed it in my jacket without a single shell spent.

The man with the fat dog looked at me. I just shrugged and waved. What could I say? The Chicken Wagon must have dropped a dozen birds off at the parking lot and driven away in a hurry to make the rounds. Catching a bird in the air seemed no different from catching his rubber ball on the bounce.

About two hundred yards down the trail, we met a cock pheasant perched on a branch about ten feet up a tree. It clucked at us. The dog ran below, barking. The stupid bird kept clucking, clearly fresh off the Chicken Wagon.

"Get out of here, Bird!" I shouted. I threw some big sticks at the nincompoop, nearly hitting him. I waved the muzzle of my gun four feet below.

I threw a few more branches at the clucking bird. Then I threw insults. He would not fly, and I would not blast him off his tree branch. Darwin would get that ditch chicken someday but not us.

We had a pleasant hike, saw some Sandhill cranes and a big doe. The gentle wind across the marsh grass smelled like baled hay, the footing easy as the weather had been dry. We found access to a huge cornfield where the farmer had granted an easement to allow for public hunting. We'd be back, the sun was ready to set.

When we butchered Havoc's bird, I found a single shotgun pellet that must have come from the old man's ruckus. I was glad Havoc retrieved the lightly wounded bird. It would not suffer for days in the field. I was proud of my dog, he was quick and strong.

A week later, we went back to the cornfield we had scouted. They had harvested the corn recently. We walked a mile with its wooded drainage ditch to our left. Thick black earth stuck to the rubber boots I had worn. The soil smelled rich and wholesome, with the faintest hint of manure. I was grateful to walk this good farmland, so different from the tangles of the marsh that were our usual fare. I sweated with the effort of unsure footing. Partly frozen slick black mud, corn stubble, and patches of frozen snow. Walking in a cornfield was rougher going than I had thought and I felt smug in my newfound knowledge.

Havoc's body language changed. Nose to the ground, his tail wagged as he wove a pattern from right to left, exploring the brush at the edge of the field. Then with a dash, chasing down the bank of the frozen channel that lined the field, and back up through thick brush, he put up a bird from the rough.

This big ring-neck was smart and experienced. He'd found a perfect spot with exposure to the sun, out of the wind, and corn from a freshly harvested field was right there. Well hidden, he had tried to run from my speedy dog before taking flight. If I was a pheasant, I would have been somewhere near that place. That's why we had walked a mile in rich muddy soil.

He fell on the harvested field on my second shot. This was a pheasant hunt, not a shotgun blasting trip to the supermarket.

*footnote: For those interested in the subtle nuances of the English language, the main collective nouns for a group of pheasants are: a bevy, a bouquet, a covey, a head, a nest or a nide (spelled: nide, nye, nie, ny). Some etymologists claim a nye should only refer to a brood of the birds.

The term 'A nye of pheasants' derives from the corruption of 'an eye', which is Old English for a brood. Delving deeper: a brood is a family of pheasants, a pair of shot birds is a brace, and a bouquet is a general gathering of pheasants. Everyone knows that a flock of crows is called 'a murder'. My on-line friend Monty contributed to my education on collective nouns. He also pointed out that one might see a 'congress of owls' or an 'exaltation of larks.' I suspect Monty wears tweeds at the gun club.

Chapter 2. Wring the Neck, Field Dress, and Age the Bird

"There's a big difference between mostly dead and all dead. Mostly dead is slightly alive. With all dead, well, with all dead there's usually only one thing you can do."

- Miracle Max, from The Princess Bride

"What do you do when the bird blinks at you after the dog returns with it?"

Wring its neck quickly to end its suffering, without making a fuss.

"But how do you wring a pheasant's neck, exactly?"

This is not a stupid question. When put to my pals on a shotgun chat-board, the answers stretched out in depth, breadth, and nonsense.

"I carry a fish billy in my jacket. It works for whacking pheasants over the head, too," one of the crew advised.

"A billy club? That seems like one extra thing to carry. I turn my hunting knife around and thwack 'em that way," a contributor rebutted.

"*I have all the lightest gear and carry the slimmest damn pocket knife I can find. Why not just wring the neck?*" You gotta love chat boards. How do I wring a pheasant's neck? Just wring its neck, that's how. Thanks a bunch.

The discussion veered off topic as members argued if pheasants were better than grouse, and how they don't make Scout knives with gut hooks anymore. A guy from Colorado started talking about Hungarian Partridge.

Out of the blue, someone typed the correct answer by mistake:

How to Wring a Pheasant's Neck

- *Hold your thumb and forefinger around the bird's neck.*
- *Let your arm hang to the side.*
- *Swing the bird in an arc to the 12:00 position, up over your head.*
- *Then pull the bird straight down. Snap your wrist up just before the bird hits the ground.*
- Like cracking a whip, this breaks the neck. Death is instantaneous. Keep holding tight. It's dead, but the wings might flap for a disturbing minute in reflexive death throes.

We've all heard about chickens running with their heads chopped off. It's upsetting the first few times. But its suffering ended.

Back on the chat board thread, some good tips were being shared.

"I had a dead cockerel run off once. I felt terrible about it."
No one likes to lose a prize, let alone cause a bird to suffer in the wild.

"A few years ago, the dead pheasant in the back of my jacket woke up. Then I had three pounds of flapping, squawking wild chicken in the small of my back. It was horrible!"
A smart hunter wrings the neck of all but the most shot up birds, just in case. Ethical hunters minimize suffering.

"Once a pheasant flushed as I was putting another in my game pouch."
Stay alert after the dog retrieves a pheasant. Your prize may have brothers hiding close in the weeds. Wring the neck, then check the immediate area for prey that may have held their flush.

"I went hunting in North Dakota and my friends would not stop and wait for me to deal with my bird." A group of hunters expects everyone to know their business when working a productive field. Wring your bird's neck, stuff it in your jacket, and field-dress it as soon as practical.

Field Dressing a Pheasant

Remove the warm, wet, heavy guts from inside the body cavity, so the meat cools quicker. Bacteria growth slows rapidly when internal meat temperature drops.

Many experienced hunters don't do this unless it's a warm day. Your author field dresses unless in a snowstorm. Pheasants have a body temperature of 105° F. Field dressing takes less than two minutes, is tidy, odor free, and helps the meat cool. Those guts need to come out at some point, anyhow.

Here's how:

- Lay the bird on its back. Grasp the long tail feathers from behind, your thumb on top, right near the bum.

- Lift the tail, exposing the *cloaca*. That's the fancy name for the pheasant's butt-hole. Birds have one orifice to pass waste, eggs or semen. That's the cloaca.

- Insert a sharp knife at the ten o'clock position. Cut a two-inch incision along the edge of the pointed rib cage. When you find the right angle, the cut will be easy to make.

- The bird's feet are up. Slide two fingers of your free hand into the incision along the top of the cavity. You will find what feels like a big golf ball. That's the gizzard.

- Curl your fingers around the gizzard and gently pull it from the body cavity. Intestines and other organs will come right out. Discard this stuff properly.

- This operation might involve a few drops of blood or a little slime. Clean your fingers by wiping them in the grass, letting your dog lick them clean, or a pat on the back of your hunting partner. This is not a messy procedure.

If you reach deep into the body cavity, you can pull out the liver. My dog receives hot bloody liver in payment for doing all the work. There are many opinions about this practice. Good or bad, your author is not a fan of liver. But maybe you are.

Reaching deeper, you could pull out the heart. Don't. Put it back in, if you do. It's great for soup.

The gizzard. It's a funny little ball of muscle filled with rocks. Real rocks. The gizzard stores pebbles pecked from the ground. It grinds up seeds and tough food before the stomach. If you don't mind a tiny fuss in preparation, it's tasty. Someday you might up your culinary experience with gizzard. Then again, maybe not.

You could dry inside the body cavity with clean paper towels, if you really want to. But dried grass, weeds or rinsing the bird in creek water spreads dangerous germs. Never spread germs!

Aging.

Hang your bird by the neck for three to five days at 50° F. or cooler. Modern science and hundreds of years of tradition agree, aged meat tastes better and is more tender. Some people think this is a controversial practice. Some people think Chicago is the capital of Illinois, too. Meat needs aging.

You're tuckered out when you get home from a long day hunting. There is a hungry dog to feed, soggy clothes to hang up, muddy boots and a gun to clean and put away. Hang your birds in a cool place (less than 50 ° F) and deal with them later.

You probably don't have a special Pheasant Hanging Refrigerator. Your bird can hang in your garage or shed, out of reach from nibbling mice. If the temperature gets much cooler, age for as long as one week, but it must not freeze. If the temperature in the storage area rises above 55° F, butcher right away.

Aged guts eventually turn smelly and disgusting. That's another reason to remove them in the field.

Hank Shaw's excellent cook book cites an Australian taste test and concludes that the temperature must be under 55 F and above 32F. Three to five days at 50-55 is good. The cooler the bird, the longer it can age. Longer than one week is pressing your luck. Natural enzymes, working at a cool temperature, do their magic.

When one must butcher a fresh bird, store the prized breast filets in the refrigerator for a few days before cooking. Enzymes will do their thing. Freeze legs, thighs and the carcass immediately. They will be slow-cooked in the future. Once you freeze meat, you must cook it when thawed. You should not freeze it again.

The Department of Primary Industries of New South Wales published it's study called "Processing Pheasant."

(https://www.dpi.nsw.gov.au/animals-and-livestock/poultry-and-birds/species/pheasant-raising/processing)

It concluded:

"In conjunction with the Consumer Education Freezing of Foods Council (NSW) preliminary trials have been conducted with taste panels using pheasant carcases which have been hung for varying periods of time from 0–11 days. For tasting purposes pheasant flesh from 18-week-old males was submitted fresh, and, after hanging for 3, 4, 6, 8, 10 or 11 days at a temperature of 15°C, the carcases were roasted in oven bags at 190°C for 1¼ hours...

All members of the panel agreed that pheasants hung for at least 3 days were more acceptable than those hung for a shorter period. Some members preferred birds to be hung for more than a week."

So, hang your prizes in a cool place, enjoy a warm meal and relaxing beverage. Put your feet up and read a book. Butcher those birds in three to five days. It's both science and tradition.

Chapter 3. Cook Each Cut of Meat the Best Way

I like pheasants. I like spotting them, or hearing their short call across a marshy field in the evening. They're not native species, but pheasants seem good to me.

I hit the brakes of the Subaru, slowing to a stop. My dog snapped to full alert as two cock pheasants crossed the highway, strutting like they owned the world. Watching from his spot in the back hatch, his eyes tracked the birds with murderous intent. They disappeared into the green spring growth along the creek.

"Good dog. Those birds are not for us."

The dog didn't make a sound, but his eyes remained locked on the ditch as we picked up speed and crossed over the small country bridge. He stared out the back window as we left the ring-necks in the weeds behind us. He knew exactly where those birds were, but didn't understand that the season closed four months ago.

Hunters have a complex relationship with their prey. Feelings of regret, gratitude, and pride cycle when we hold that pheasant we just shot. Soft, warm and smelling of clean musk.

We'll feel regret as we cut, tear, skin and butcher this beautiful bird. But taking life without using the meat the best way possible would be a sin.

Pheasants are running birds. They can fly, but mostly they run. Their strong legs beg for long simmering. Two or three hours in tomato sauce, wine sauce, or as a base for soup will do it. Then they are sweet and fall-off-the-bone tender. You can easily remove unpleasant drumstick tendons when butchering.

Tender breast filets are the premier cut. These cook in six to eight minutes. The biggest culinary danger is cooking a breast filet one minute too long. Baked, they might cook as long as twenty minutes in a poaching liquid.

The remaining carcass and giblets make soup. Not just any soup, but delicious home-made pheasant soup.

Some fellows take forty minutes to pluck a bird naked. They create an enormous pile of feathers, and the difficult problem of cooking breast and legs at the same time. A talented chef can do it, but why?

A better way to prepare and cook pheasant.

Skin the breast from the feathers, making two breast filets. Pull the drumstick tendons, then skin and break the legs and thighs free.

The prized breast filets are best eaten fresh within a few days after butchering. Grilled, fried or baked. Cooking times are brief. If fortune is good or timing unlucky, breasts can be frozen, separate from all other cuts of the bird.

Legs and thighs—freeze them right away. Those weeks will come when luck is thin, then it's time to thaw and slow cook them for dinner. Some small bones, a few tendons and some tough connecting tissues will be found, but guests can easily pick tender leg meat clean with a fork. Set small side plates for discarded bones or the occasional shotgun pellet. It's part of the exotic nature of eating wild game.

Freeze the carcass, neck and giblets separately. When it's time, make pheasant soup.

Breasts, legs, and carcass are all best cooked in different ways. So let's take the bird apart and store those cuts of meat separately. Sometimes, working smarter is better than working harder.

Chapter 4. Butchering. From Bird to Meat—How to Skin a Pheasant.

I'm not good at plucking pheasants, pheasant plucking I get stuck. Though some peasants find it pleasant I'd much rather pluck a duck.

   Oh, but plucking geese is gorgeous, I can pluck a goose with ease, but plucking pheasants is sheer torture, for they haven't any grease.

   - The Pheasant Plucker's Son, Traditional Old English Rhyme

Plucking a pheasant is a boring process that makes a big mess. There's a better way. Skinning takes less than ten minutes. Fifteen minutes to show a new fella, and half an hour if the dog helps.

The first steps we'll do on the back porch. Keep the pooch in the house. I've got a pheasant aged about three to five days, and the loop of twine it hung from.

The string is important. Twenty-four inches of twine, tied with a generous overhand knot. Let me show you.

First Stage: Skinning. An Outside Job.

Sorry, Bird, but your head comes off. I crunch neck bones with the anvil garden pruners (pruning shears) pulled from my back pocket.

Feathers are tough, so it takes a quick swipe with a sharp knife to finish the job. Plunk! Head in the rubbish.

Next, snare the bird's ankles together with that loop of string. Put the string around the ankles for later.

On the deck, I spread the wings, then lay the bird on its back. Positioning one heel on an 'armpit', then the other. The pheasant is anchored to the ground.

Your toes point in the same direction as the neck, heels tight against the body. Use your heels, not toes. Trust me.

I bend over, slip one hand through the loop of twine and grab both of the bird shins with both hands. Then I pull. Harder and harder.

OOF. Gotta keep pulling. This loop of twine around my wrist is taking the strain; I don't need the grip strength of a professional arm wrestler. And... there we go!

Something gives way in the bird. It's the lower spine separating. I stand up straight, the bird's scaly feet, legs and pelvis in my hands. A pink skinned pheasant breast rests between my ankles.

I place the legs on top of my gas grill. It just happens to be closer than the picnic table.

Cupping my hands to keep the feathers away from this nice meat, I pick it up. A few crunches with garden shears, about an inch from the armpits, and the wings fall in the trash.

A stout pair of kitchen scissors is well worth the price. They cost about the same as a dozen shotgun shells. But a knife and cutting board will work, too. Snipping, I set the trimmed carcass on a platter next to the long, thin neck. The neck is excellent soup meat, save it.

Now turn your attention to those legs. Some say the thighs taste better than the breasts. But the drumstick has many bone-like sinews which must be removed now.

Picking up the lower half of the torn bird, I press one shin bone against a post on my back porch, breaking the leg above the spur. Use the edge of a table, a fence post, a sapling... anything hard to push against. Then twirl the broken bone around.

The foot and ankle are only held to the drumstick by strong tendons. Snare the single broken foot with the twine. The loop goes around the foot, then pull the knot through it, snugging to make a handle.

I put the loop of twine, now holding the bird's foot, over a hook on the house. A hammock goes there in the summer. You might use a doorknob, tree branch or anything sturdy. You can even slip your foot into the loop if you're young and spry. Then pull.

Grasping the drumstick firmly in both hands, I pull... Squeeeeak! Six long white tendons slide from the drumstick. The foot looks like a tiny white chicken-foot cat o' nine tails. I give the other leg the same treatment.

With a loop of twine I already have, the job is effortless. I saw a fellow on YouTube pin the broken foot between his boot heel and a brick. I tried, and ended up red-faced and bug-eyed, pulling with all my might, tottering on one heel. It didn't work for me. Come hunting season, all the bricks are wet, frozen, or covered in snow anyway.

This loop of twine is magic.

Holding the deboned drumstick, I trim at the feather line with garden shears. Then, I push the leg towards the hip. A meaty knee appears. I hook a finger behind this knee, peel the leg free of the feathered skin, then pop the femur free of the hip socket.

Hold the bare leg and carcass. Press the hip joint backward against a table edge. Once it separates, I snip the meat close to the pelvis with scissors. The thigh and leg are free from the body. A knife would work, too.

After removing the second leg, the job is almost done. Our platter holds two legs with tendons removed, a neck, and a pale pink pheasant chest.

I pluck the longest brown and black striped tail feather from the lightweight, meatless lower carcass. It's a souvenir. Then I throw the wad of ex-pheasant in the trash.

A few tiny stray down feathers swirl in the wind on the porch. That's the extent of the mess. Now we take our rough butchered meat inside.

Final Butchering: Filet, Clean and Freeze.

The kitchen area around the sink was cleaned and wiped with a bleach solution or antibacterial spray. That's the same as working with any raw meat.

I set a roll of paper towels, a cutting board, and two clean plates next to the sink.

Inside the carcass, I find the heart, remove it, rinse, and trim the little white valves off. Wipe it across a paper towel to dry, and set it on a plate. "It's great for soup. Once cut up, you won't

Rinse the carcass with cold running water. Set it 'keel up' on a cutting board. Grab a sharp boning knife. Cut straight down alongside the center bone, skillfully peeling meat from the keel. Keep the sharp edge against bone as you work. Pull and cut like a surgeon to remove one breast filet.

The smaller muscle nestled there is called the 'tender', try to keep it together with the breast.

Rinse the filet clean, then drag it across a paper towel to clean and dry. Put it on a clean plate. When the other filet has joined, cover them in plastic wrap and put in the refrigerator. We eat these gems first, cooking within five days. Since they are already aged, we could make them into a dinner treat tonight.

A narrow-bladed kitchen knife is called a 'boning knife.' Don't laugh. It's not as flexible as a fish filet knife, but handier than a hunting knife. Don't worry about meat left on the carcass, your filleting skills will improve with practice. Nothing is wasted. That carcass will make fantastic soup.

Rinse the carcass, and neck, wipe and set them next to the heart to drain and dry. Put the carcass, neck and giblets of up to three birds in one freezer bag, if lucky enough to have that bounty. I roll a little paper towel cigar, slip it in the bag near the zipper, and seal the bag with only a little air. The paper towel will help absorb some moisture. Into the freezer they go. This bag is now ready kit to make one amazing soup. Repeat, rinsing the legs, freezing them separately.

The most flexible way to store legs is by the number of people having dinner. I freeze them in pairs; it's just me and my wife now. When legs are cooked, the correct number can go frozen into steaming hot sauces.

A kitchen pro would label each bag and date them. I like to be professional, but my wife has warned about boring my friends. Details about Sharpie markers are obvious, so I'll keep quiet and refrain from preaching about reusing the freezer bags.

Give the kitchen, cutting boards and tools a mighty good cleaning with hot water, soap and anti-bacterial spray.

The only question is: how do you want to cook those amazing breast filets? I have recipes.

Useful Tidbits:

SHOT UP BIRDS.

Pheasants often arrive with a broken wing. If the 'stand-and-pull' won't work, rip the skin from the breast using your fingers. It's not elegant, but it gets the job done.

No matter how shot up, some meat can always be salvaged. Save what you can. Aim for the head next time and work with your partners so you don't all blast the same bird. A mangled breast can be used for soup, or Pheasant Salad or Quiche recipes.

WOUND CHANNELS.

Red lines in pink meat are trails of a lead pellet to track down. Pull out feathers embedded in flesh, rinse and wipe the meat clear of blood. A round, hard, fuzzy ball is a pellet with a feather wrapped around it.

Shot can escape our most thorough inspection, so warn guests to cut food into small morsels and chew carefully. They can turn in a pellet for extra dessert, finding one at dinner is good luck.

GREENING.

Meat near a wound channel might color light green. This is uncommon, but it's not serious. Bacteria created Hydrogen Sulfide. Spoiled meat should be trimmed and discarded. Wipe the edge of the good meat with a vinegar soaked cloth and carry on; the remainder is good.

FREEZING.

Never allow uncooked meat to freeze twice. On an arctic hunt, whole birds must not freeze before butchering. In extreme cold, it may not be possible to age a bird by hanging. Butcher right away. Breast filets should sit three days in the refrigerator before cooking.

EASY LEG PULLS.

Break the lower backbone with pruning shears, snip just above the gray triangle of feathers at the bird's tail. The breast will separate far more easily now.

Tools and Supplies for Preparing Fowl:

- Sharp hunting style knife
- Cutting board

- Loop made from 2 feet of sturdy twine
- Sharp kitchen boning knife or large paring knife
- Platter or large plate
- Small trash bag
- Paper towels
- Gallon sized zip-lock freezer bags
- Kitchen Plates
- Spray kitchen cleaning solution

- Sturdy kitchen scissors or game shears. Highly recommended.
- Anvil style garden pruning shears. Any garden shears are worth their weight in gold.

Skinning is easy, quick and clean. You have saved each cut of meat separately, waiting to be cooked in the best way for their nature.

Chapter 5. Christmas Birds

"My dad says you should go shoot a couple of pheasants," my wife informed me.

"What?" I sputtered. "Does he have any idea what he's asking?"

"He wants Pheasant Under Glass for Christmas dinner. He and Doris are driving up from Indiana. I've been telling them on Zoom about the meals you've been cooking."

"Shoot a couple pheasants, like it's going to the supermarket?" My eyebrows raised. "I don't even know what Pheasant Under Glass is, and Christmas is five days away. I don't want to disappoint them."

"Don't worry. Take the dog hunting tomorrow. I have faith in you two." She hugged her dumbfounded husband and rubbed the dog's ear before retiring to her office.

The dog looked at me because someone said 'hunting'. Dogs are amazing. They can memorize up to two hundred and fifty words. That's more than some of my relatives. The recipe online for Pheasant Under Glass looked complicated. I expected the fancy glass serving dish, but not morel mushrooms.

I woke early the next morning with an uneasy feeling. The old-fashioned cotton suspenders of my field pants slipped over my wicking undershirt. My fleece sweater went on before I slipped downstairs in expensive wool-blend socks.

The dog wolfed down a cup of kibble before I could get my second boot on, so it wasn't easy to tie the laces with a wiggle-waggle Labrador budging my elbow.

Canvas field jacket, orange upland vest and hat, shells, shotgun. I ran a mental checklist before opening the car's hatchback. When it came to pheasants, three-year-old Havoc was capable, but he was still learning to jump into the car. I lifted him with a grunt. Then I could hear his tail thumping as we drove south. The hint of pink sunrise to the east faded upwards into a robin's egg blue winter sky.

We were getting better at pheasant hunting, nearing the end of our second season in the field. We explored a large hunting ground close to home, with increasing luck. Oak forest, stands of tall hilltop pines, prairie grass plains and miles of marshland ankle deep in standing water. There was something new to discover with every trip.

Last winter, I followed cross-country ski tracks through the thick forest. They led to a wide tractor trail, which passed a meandering trout stream with icy banks. The trail cut hard to the right for half a mile, then ended at a solitary unmarked steel gate to a lonesome country road. That became our secret entrance to remote public hunting land.

We drove on a little-known country road to an obscure gravel parking circle. It serviced a portion of Wisconsin's Ice Age Trail. A few hundred yards down the road was our innocent looking locked gate. Soon, the dog was pulling hard at his leash towards the path that led to secret territories.

Open fields to our right. Rough bush to our left, with tangles upon tangles of thick invasive honeysuckle. Walking on the tarmac, I marveled at how many times we had gotten lost in that tall brush. Attempts to follow deer paths led to disorientation and ruin. A true outdoorsman would have found his way, or maybe he'd avoid bush only a tenderfoot would attempt.

We were smarter now and walked on the pavement.

Honeysuckle, thorny bramble, buckthorn, Canadian thistle, and burdock. That thicket was a combination of nature's most horrible five plants. They poke, scratch, tear and trip a man.

Lost in that stubborn maze, I found myself in calf-deep water at one point, but never found that marsh again. Thorn covered vines had picked my orange hat from my head as I ducked under them. They snagged a glove from my pocket once, and tore my clothes as I pushed through sideways. Any adversity could be found in there, with no clear path or room to turn around.

Discretion being the better part of valor, we walked down the civilized road to the orange, four rail heavy duty steel farm gate.

Memories of my father came to mind. The shotgun under my arm was an Ithaca, like his had been. He was old, and time had been unkind. First it had taken his mental acuity, then personality, and finally his mobility. Fifteen years ago, he would have loved to walk in the fields with me and my good dog. He would have understood if I said, "Pheasant hunting is not about shooting birds." Much of hunting is about dogs, who have been doing this dance with men since before civilization. It's why Labradors exist—nearly thirty thousand years of selective breeding.

The cherished shotgun under my arm was blued metal and hand rubbed walnut, selected with utmost care to run smooth, and shoot where I looked. I knew every dimension within a hair, even an extra sweater alters my swing. Bird hunting is why shotguns exist, too.

We explored open prairie, marsh, and forest edges in crisp autumn sunshine, fog, sleet or snow. The dog and I knew this land. What we didn't know, we scouted. Animals, plants, and long-lost artifacts like the rusting mule plow we had discovered in the middle of the marsh. It must have belonged to farmers that failed 80 years ago. A mouse, a hawk, a deflated wedding balloon hanging on a branch. No one but us would see these things today. We packed out the deflated balloon in my pocket.

Three shells pushed into the Ithaca. The strange feeling of needing a pair of birds nagged at me. With my in-laws visiting our home for the first time, I felt somehow the Christmas dinner would impress them with my worth, and Felicia would look good in their eyes. I needed two birds.

We started our hunt, edging past the orange gate, the lone marker to an old gravel road that was overgrown with weeds. The trail passed through a large open field cut into a mixed forest. Hoary frost sparkled as the morning sun made steam rise from the lowlands. The path took us past the bend in the stream where the dog always got a drink, then through the tunnel of tall, arching, leafless branches. It rose over the top of a rocky knoll, and under the windswept gnarled white oak which pointed to the abandoned apple trees in the dell. It ended in an enormous field, surrounded by stands of aspen, green pines, and winter oak. Islands of underbrush offered untold edge habitat, the environment deer and pheasants seem to prefer.

The dog had not scented a bird, so I worried this hunt might come up short. My stomach was tight as I thought about failing my wife.

Then the dog put his nose to the trail. His body grew stiff, tail wagged, and snuffling the thin snow, he dashed away, then darted back. I saw a pheasant track in the snow, big three-pronged fork with the cross members bent forward. The dog was trailing the wrong way. A quick three whistles and he was charging back, nose to the ground, past me in a flash.

With drumming wings and wild cackling, a golden brown bird with brilliant green and red head flushed in front of the dog. My first shot was hasty and wide. I don't recall mounting the gun or pumping the action. Second shot, the bird spiraled to the earth near the edge of the forest; the dog bounded underneath in chase. Havoc vanished behind a hedge of rough underbrush. The sound of a Labrador crashing about like a small bulldozer broke the silence after the gunshots.

"Havoc!" I called. "Havoc, fetch it!" Taking a few steps in his direction, and keeping an eye on where the bird fell, I wondered what was keeping him. "Havoc!"

My fox-red Labrador appeared, tail and head held high, trotting through an opening in the brush. The enormous pheasant in his mouth was fighting. The bird beat his face with a wing and wriggled free, but Havoc pounced and had him again. With a shake of his head and all the pride in the world, he trotted to hold the bird at my feet.

"Good dog!" Havoc gave me his prize, panting and grinning. His cheek had two bloody scratches under it. He could not have looked happier. I grabbed the blue-green, white ringed neck. The bird flapped its wings in reflexive spasm, then I chided Havoc for giving it one last little nip. "I've got him. Leave it."

The dog capered with excitement, jumping into the air but never touching me.

For a while, I thought his favorite thing was to fetch a ball. Then I thought it was to leap from a dock and swim like an otter to bring that ball back. Flushing a pheasant was much better, but it took most of the previous season to gather my rhythm and bring down a flying bird. Bringing back a fighting bird after finding, flushing, and chasing it down was what made him prance.

The bleeding red scratches on his cheek meant nothing to him. He was a proud veteran upland retriever in his mind. This was his first battle, and he was only two years old, with much training yet to come. I worried my wife would kill me for bringing the dog back all marked up.

Havoc earned the pay for his labor, warm bloody liver from the field dressed bird. He gulped it down, licking my fingers clean. It was a beautiful big cock pheasant with a grand long tail. Its feathers were soft, and smelled wholesome, with a slight musk as I stowed it in the back pocket of my hunting vest.

We'd walked a fair way for our first bird. The sun would set early this far north, and so near the solstice. I felt the cold in my bones. There was a large rough meadow left to hunt, but something told me it was a good time to start back for the car. Everything had gone to plan, no point in tempting fate. It was cold.

The dog was on high alert, double checking every sniff. He stayed close, for the most part, which was a recent improvement. Maybe he was staying closer because of the treats in my generous pocket. My young dog was hunting at proper distances. I didn't need to call him back with constant whistles.

Havoc put his nose to trail and dove into the weeds. A big golden pheasant burst into flight with the cackles and drumming wings that ignited fantasy and surprise. Swinging from right to left, the bird was a classic skeet shot, one I had practiced often many years ago. The gun sounded, and the bird went down, right into the middle of an enormous thick island of honeysuckle and buckthorn. "Oh crap. Find your bird, Havoc!"

He didn't hesitate. In he went, crawling under a fallen tree branch. No sounds, nothing. I waded through the tall grass to the edge of the tangle. "Havoc! Find it!" I called, but was not hopeful he could bring anything back through such thick underbrush. A minute passed. "Havoc!"

I whistled three times, and the sound echoed through the silent woods. I could see nothing in the morass of small, dense growth. "Havoc!" He appeared to my right, a pheasant held gently in his mouth. He'd found a way out and then circled to find me. Another large beauty. This one had not put up a fight. A well placed crossing shot is often what we strive for, a dead bird in the air. Tired, the wonderful dog lay down as he surrendered his find.

We had our daily limit, two large pheasants, their long brown striped tail feathers sticking from my jacket. I arrange them that way, for fashion. The walk back to the car was easy for me, but Havoc didn't understand the idea of a daily limit or that dinner had been assured. He checked every likely spot, all the way to the parking lot, then slept soundly on the drive home.

"How'd it go?" Felicia asked, looking over the top of her book and holding out her hand. She was near the fire, sitting across from the Christmas tree.

The dog trotted over to bump her palm with his nose. "We got two," I told her.

"I told you not to worry."

We had Grilled Maple and Apple Pheasant with Minnesota Wild Rice and Acorn Squash for Christmas. The in-laws were impressed. My wife was happy, and the dog watched from his rug in the kitchen.

Someone may have said, "you should write a cookbook."

Notes

Grilled Apple/Maple Pheasant Breast, Wild Rice and Acorn Squash

Chapter 6. A Grilled Feast:

Grilled Apple/Maple Pheasant Breast, Wild Rice and Acorn Squash

Guests are sure to be impressed by the wild game and locally sourced ingredients. Paired with the satisfying flavor combination of grilled pheasant and apple,

An excellent cook uses fresh ingredients, and fresh ingredients make a mediocre cook look great. The flavors pop. Textures are crunchy when they should be crisp, and smooth when they should be soft. It's worth finding better produce when cooking special meals. Let's make use of foods sourced locally from the Midwest.

Things to know/ why this works

Breast filets are delicate, with subtle deep flavor unlike other fowl. The butchering might not be professional yet, but you supervised every step of its journey from wild bird to beautiful pink meat.

The autumn harvest includes cherries, wild rice, apples, squash, and maple syrup. The timing and flavors of these ingredients are perfect for cooking with wild game.

Wild rice grows in shallow lakes and slow streams. It's hearty and flavorful. Minnesota is famous for this distant cousin of white rice, and I always pick some up at a roadside stand when in that state. We'll be adding some tart chopped dried cherries from Michigan.

Acorn squash, one of the smallest gourds, is also the most flavorful. It grows throughout the Midwest. With butter, brown sugar and maple syrup, eating healthy never tasted so good and the hour long bake is worth the wait.

Various states vie for supremacy, yet any real maple syrup, direct from a local producer, is superior to Name Brands. Counterfeit sweeteners go into that bulk stuff, no matter what they claim on the bottle. Maple syrup and butter come from Wisconsin. We can fight about the best liquid gold, but not the butter.

Gourmet chunky applesauce is essential for grilling and serving as a side dish. Search your local farmers' market or fancy foods isle for rough cut chunks of apple in a Mason jar. It's made in small batches, maybe by someone's mom.

The Elegant Farmer of Mukwonogo, Wi. offers a delicious product for about $10 per 16-ounce jar (in 2023.) That's three times the price of production applesauce and worth every penny. Using regular applesauce, you're a good cook. With **gourmet cinnamon applesauce**, you're a bold, cutting-edge world class chef. Believe it will work and dare to try.

If you can't find something that's close to being homemade, add your own apple chunks to the best factory applesauce you can buy. Cooks with real home-made applesauce in the cupboard are golden.

This meal is all about the fresh local flavors of early winter, and the fun of off-season grilling. Yes, man cooks with fire, sometimes in the snow. There is nothing wrong with a propane grill in December.

Three minutes per side for a pheasant breast fillet. A moment of overcooking and it's dry and tough. Trust the timer and the poke test. Poke test? Poke the tip of your nose, then the meat. They should both offer the same firmness and resistance.

The USDA says to use a meat thermometer to measure an internal temperature of 165° F. Very thick filets (three quarters of an inch thick from an enormous wild cock pheasant) may take an extra forty-five seconds per side. It's difficult to use a meat thermometer on these thin filets, while on a hot grill. I trust the finger poke test.

The recipes for Apple/Maple Pheasant, Wild Rice with Cherries and Maple Acorn Squash follow.

Squash will be in the oven for one hour, the wild rice requires forty-five minutes on the stove. The pheasant needs only six minutes on the grill. While the squash and rice can warm for fifteen minutes after cooking, serve the pheasant immediately.

Pair with Pinot Gris/Pinot Grigio (dry white wine), Champaigne, Cider (alcoholic, a dryer variety), lager style craft beer, and/or mineral water. Man also enjoy nice glass of wine with meal.

Chapter 6.1 Recipe: Grilled Apple/Maple Pheasant

Serves: 2 Preparation: 45 minutes Cook: 6 minutes

Quick, easy, and delicious without cleanup. I use my gas grill year-round, even if it means shoveling a path through the snow to get to it.

Ingredients:

- Two pheasant breast filets, skinned. (3 to 5 ounces, each)
- 8 ounces gourmet cinnamon chunky applesauce (or regular)
- 1 crisp, tart apple
- 3 tablespoons real maple syrup
- 1 tablespoon apple cider vinegar.

Lets get cooking.

o Marinate the breast filets with 3 tablespoons maple syrup and 1 tablespoon apple cider vinegar. Add another *teaspoon* or two vinegar to the marinade for a more tangy taste. Paint the filets. Let soak, covered, in the refrigerator for forty-five minutes.

If serving regular, non-specialty apple sauce, dice half a crisp tart apple into one-eighth inch chunks. Mix into 8 ounces of regular applesauce. Refrigerate. Use gourmet applesauce straight from the jar.

- o Preheat grill to medium high heat, 400-425° F.
- o Brush the grate clean and place filets on the grill. Let cook on covered grill for exactly three minutes.
- o Flip the filets. Meat will be pink, tender, and have black grill marks. Plop a large dollop (about 2 tablespoons) of gourmet cinnamon applesauce atop each.
- o Cover grill and cook for 3 more minutes.

- o Use the finger poke test to verify the meat is cooked. Overcooking is the most common error. Remove meat from heat, allow to rest for two minutes.

Plate with applesauce and sliced apple garnish. Wild rice and Acorn Squash recipes follow.

This is a favorite technique for pheasant breast. If lucky enough to have more fillets than guests, pheasant salad and pheasant quiche are easy and delicious use of leftovers.

Chapter 6.2 Recipe: Wild Rice with Cherries

Serves: 2 Preparation: 5 minutes Cooking: 45 minutes

Wild rice has a rich, earthy flavor. We add ¼ cup chopped dried cherries for a tart sweet contrasting element.

Other options: 1/8 cup chopped crispy bacon, toasted pine nuts, or toasted salted walnuts. ¼ cup of fresh, very firm chopped peach is a nod to the South.

Substitute one tablespoon of olive oil for a tablespoon of butter, if desired.

Be bold and proud of local flavors.

Use half a chicken boullion cube in water or 2 cups of chicken broth. Your choice.

Ingredients

- 1 cup wild rice
- ½ chicken boullion cube
- 1 tablespoon butter
- ¼ cup dried cherries.

Lets get cooking

- o Bring 2 cups water in a medium sized saucepan to a boil. Dissolve ½ cube of chicken boullion.

- o Rinse the wild rice in clear cold water, strain, then add to saucepan.

- o Immediately lower heat and let simmer for 45 minutes.

- o Drain cooked rice, fluff with fork. Stir in 1/4 cup chopped cherries and 1 tablespoon butter.

The rich flavors and chewy texture of this ancient grain, combined with tart cherries, is really something special.

Chapter 6.3 Recipe: Maple Acorn Squash

Serves: 2 Preparation: 5 minutes Cooking: 45 minutes

Acorn squash, also known as pepper squash or Des Moines squash, is round, green, and has wide vertical ridges. The orange flesh is among the most flavorful of the squashes.

Ingredients:

- 1 Acorn squash
- 2 tablespoons brown sugar
- 2 tablespoons buttermilk
- 1 tablespoon maple syrup
- ¼ teaspoon sage (optional)

Lets get cooking.

- Preheat the oven to 400° F.

- Cut the green acorn squash in half, lengthwise with a large, sturdy, sharp chef's knife and much force.

- Scoop the seeds with a spoon and discard them.

- Cut a crosshatch pattern in the flesh of the squash. Use deep cuts, three quarters of an inch apart.

- Smear a tablespoon of butter into each half, then sprinkle 1 tablespoon of brown sugar into each, then a teaspoon of maple syrup. Massage into the flesh of the squash with fingertips. Optional: sprinkle a pinch of sage over each.

- Grease a *rimmed* cookie sheet or large baking pan with cooking spray, shortening or parchment paper for easy cleanup. Place the acorn squash flesh up, skin down.

A flat cookie sheet allows liquid to drip into the hot oven with a negative outcome.

- Bake for one hour at 400° F.

This is so good you must never let guests know it's easy to prepare.

Chapter 7. Clear, with a Chance of Afternoon Snow Flurries

I got a marvelous piece of string for Christmas. My daughter Jane had put cookies, candies, baking mixes and a cooking mandolin under the Christmas tree. I liked my carefully wrapped presents and admired the attractive four-ply jute twine which held them in a bundle. Good string. I put it in my pocket.

The next day, my wife said, "You should take the dog hunting. He's driving me crazy." So I looked up the weather report for the next day: "Clear, with a chance of light snow flurries in the afternoon." Excellent.

I love my wife. She's nearly perfect, always right and has the nicest way of telling me when I am underfoot. Unlike fishing or going after deer, pheasant hunters rarely crawl out of bed before the crack of dawn. The dog and I set off at a civilized ten o'clock the next morning.

It's a half hour drive to the marsh. I contemplated the dark featureless sky through the windshield as we drove. The weather was not clear. The strong gusting wind caused my car to swerve occasionally, and the sun was completely hidden.

Cold, biting north wind greeted me as I stepped out for the hunt. I had worn snow boots and thick trousers, wicking synthetic long underwear, a thick poly sweater, and a hunting jacket with orange shoulders. An orange knit toque was pulled over my green Elmer Fudd hat with flaps over the ears, a red wool scarf and leather gloves completed the ensemble. The Weather Service had promised clear skies, but the conditions were nasty and unrelenting.

The dog didn't care. Oblivious to the cold and wind, he ran free. The snow was coming down sideways, so he sprinted about the unplowed parking area and returned with bright eyes, wagging tail, and a happy grin. That dog had energy to burn after too much time indoors. Eight inches of fluffy white stuff on the ground meant fun for a Labrador.

I shoved three Federal Number Fives into my Fabarms, then hurried after the dog. Fumbling to get my gloves on, I doubted the sanity of this hunt. Nature was serving up a good old-fashioned snowstorm, blowing in from the Arctic Circle with enough force to make a snowman shiver.

Wet, heavy flakes made for nearly white-out conditions. Ice stuck to my eyelashes as I squinted against the bitter wind and chose a straight path to follow, even though I could not always see it. The track paralleled a few strands of rusted barbed wire and scrub which you might call a fence. It separated a long corn field from a broad marsh.

Pheasants like edges and they like corn. This fence line faced a rising sun, if we could have seen the sun. It would have been a textbook location, except for the blizzard.

A dog can't scent a bird in twenty miles an hour of wind. Driving snow makes it worse. Moving to keep warm, I kept going, scowling under my scarf. Just to prove me wrong, the dog's behavior soon changed. He ran back and forth, nose to the snow on the ground. Back and forth, farther and farther along the trail. It wasn't easy to keep up with him. The snow was over the top of my boots as I ran.

Thirty yards away, a pheasant flushed from his snow cave. Grass and brambles had formed a little tepee that nature had covered with eight inches of insulation. Havoc found him anyway.

I set my feet. The swing of the gun was instinctive, then my new shotgun sounded and a big ring-neck cratered into a fluffy flat white field. The dog drove his head deep into the snow moments later. Despite the poor visibility, I could make out the large, golden treasure he had grabbed.

An upland Labrador finds the bird and makes it fly. The hunter shoots it, then the dog brings it back. That's the deal. Havoc could not do his job for two weeks. He'd been cooped up at home, making do with city walks and clandestine treats from my daughter. He'd been nudging my hand with his nose every few hours and driving my wife crazy, longing to explore beyond the confines of civilization.

He looked up with his bird. Our eyes met in the distance. He crouched, leapt, and sprinted back to me, the very model of a perfect gun dog. Then he put on an extra burst of speed and ran past like a freight train. Striding out his gallop over the deep snow, the pheasant still in his mouth, Havoc seemed to fly over the deep drifts. I watched as he circled me, his movements graceful and fluid.

Mouth open. I could make out the speeding wild wolf spirit. He was forty yards out, a dark blur in the white noise of the blizzard. It must have been a good thirty seconds before he turned sharply and charged, skidding to a stop at my feet. He looked up with bright brown eyes, doglike again, tail wagging madly. He had taken a victory lap.

I wrung the neck, although I doubt it was necessary. Dropping to both knees in a depression stomped in the snow, I field dressed our catch with frozen fingers and a cheap Dollar Store Chinese folding knife from my dad. The hot liver, dripping a few drops of ruby red, was offered as payment for a job well done.

With the fowl stowed, we were coming home victorious. That dog's nose dumbfounded me. The snowstorm was so thick that I could barely see a few feet ahead, but Havoc managed to find a pheasant.

"You're a nut!" I praised Havoc and patted his flank as we labored back to the car. He monitored the long tail feathers that stuck from the back pocket of my field jacket. Bouncing in the snow with an occasional spinning jump, he was full of joy from doing his job. The extreme weather was simply an interesting challenge for him to solve. The dog had done his job and I had done mine.

A few weeks past I let the team down with poor shooting, so I was feeling pretty smug about my single shot.

When we got home, I cut two feet of jute twine from my pocket and fashioned it into a loop to hang the pheasant in the garage. The sound of kibble hitting the bowl distracted the dog, giving me a moment to thaw out before putting my gear away.

My wife called down from her office, "Hey, look! It's snowing outside."

Chapter 8. Pasta Sauce in a Jar... How to Pick a Good One

Tomato sauce serves as the base for grilled or fried pheasant breast over pasta, or as a simmering sauce for legs. If you know what to look for, store-bought sauce can be as good as home-made. Really.

My Grandmother immigrated from Italy, got married and had 12 children. My mom helped make pasta and sauce for fourteen, nearly every day, until she escaped by getting married. She only had four kids.

"I don't apologize for sauce in a jar anymore," my mother said as she poured a jar of Ragu into a deep frying pan. "Store-bought sauce is pretty good, especially if you're not cooking for a family." She meant a family of fourteen. She separated two cloves of garlic from a golf ball sized cluster and set them on her wooden cutting board.

WHACK.

She hit the little cloves with her wooden kitchen mallet, blew the paper-like skin away, then scraped the crushed firm remains into the pot. My mom loved that mallet. She diced a quarter of a softball sized yellow onion for the pot then added a palm full of dried oregano, a smaller amount of basil and a pinch of white sugar.

"Sugar is to control acidity. Don't use too much. And never use a metal spoon. Italian women use wooden spoons." She stirred the pot. It would simmer for half an hour.

"So sauce from a jar is pretty good. If you add garlic, onion, oregano, basil and a pinch of sugar?" I asked.

Mom was still buying the same sauce since the nineteen-fifties. Nowadays, you can buy one ready to go.

Don't Apologize for Sauce from a Jar

You'll be overwhelmed by a dizzying array of pasta sauces on the shelf of the supermarket. But how do you pick a sauce worthy of your pheasant?

Look at the ingredients: tomatoes, water, onions, olive oil, tomato paste, garlic, salt, black pepper, basil. You know what those ingredients are. That's a good sauce.

You don't want the cheapest offering. When you read: high fructose corn syrup, modified soybean anything, powdered stuff, vegetable fiber, 'natural flavoring', or chemicals you can't pronounce, these ingredients tell you to pick another.

'Natural flavors' are defined by the US Food and Drug administration to be "the essential oil, oleoresin, essence or extractive, protein hydrolysate, distillate, or any product of roasting, heating or enzymolysis, which contains the flavoring constituents derived from a spice, fruit or fruit juice, vegetable or vegetable juice, edible yeast, herb, bark, bud, root, leaf or similar plant material…"

If the factory buys 'natural flavor' from someone else, they don't need to disclose the synthetic solvents, preservatives, emulsifiers, carriers and other additives which go into making 'natural flavor'. Ha. Natural flavor, indeed.

Consider what you've spent on food for the dog. Don't be a cheapskate at the supermarket.

Chapter 9. Fresh or Artisanal Pasta

Use ingredients that reflect the pride and effort that went into getting your bird.

Fresh pasta is a giant step above spaghetti noodles from a box. It's found in the refrigerated section of your grocery store. Noodles come in many variations: regular, green spinach, roasted red pepper, gluten-free cauliflower, and many others. All are great, bold choices. Ravioli or tortellini make excellent options, too.

They sell dried gourmet linguine or fettuccine in festive wads or long crazy folded bunches. It adds an extra level to any meal. In the gravest emergency, spaghetti from a long narrow box will do. Your pheasant elevates even the humblest pasta to minor nobility. Fresh and dried artisanal pastas cook in two to three minutes. Round stuff from a box might take 12 minutes.

Test for chewiness a minute or so before the time suggested on the package. 'Al dente' means "to the tooth" in Italian, and that's how pasta is cooked—to the level you feel is done, and not much farther. Beware of overcooked pasta.

Drain pasta in a colander (pasta strainer) but never rinse with water. My Italian grandmother would hit you with a wooden spoon for that. Keep them from sticking by folding a teaspoon of olive oil into the drained noodles.

Chapter 10. Crazy Simple Marinara Sauce

Marinara Sauce Almost from Scratch. This recipe is so easy it hurts.

Things to know/ why this works

The key ingredient is whole, peeled, canned tomatoes. This is not the time to economize, buy the best. They will simmer while you lazily break the soft tomatoes against the bottom of the pot with a potato masher, or firmly against the side with a wooden spoon.

Stirring and crushing every fifteen minutes, for over an hour, there is no hurry to get them all at once. Avoid disturbing the halves of an onion that will be in the pot, too.

About that onion: get a nice big yellow one. Cut it in half, through the equator. Peel the flaky skin and first few tough 'tunic rings' off.

These halves go straight into the pot, with no further chopping, slicing, or tearful dicing. They simmer with the tomatoes for an hour, then are pulled out, and thrown away. *This sounds like the punchline from an old joke about cooking woodchucks, but this is for real.* The onion has seasoned the sauce, its job is done.

Use unsalted butter. Processed ingredients often have too much salt. A guest can always add more. Fresh, coarse ground seasoning at the table provides more flavor. And a good cook always adds salt to taste, not by teaspoons.

Chapter 10.1b Recipe: Cedar Plank Woodchuck.

Serves: 1 Preparation: this is a joke! Cooks: ignore

This is an old joke about how tough a woodchuck is.

Gut and skin woodchuck, bind it to a cedar plank with butcher's twine.

Rub the carcass with salt, pepper, garlic, and butter.

Roast at 325° for two and a half hours.

Throw away woodchuck, eat the cedar plank.

In case of a zombie apocalypse or other end-of-the-world scenario, the following information might be handy:

The woodchuck has scent glands around the armpits, genitals, and along the back. They must be removed quickly.

Brine the carcass overnight to draw out musky flavor. It can be marinated overnight again, in buttermilk, to tenderize.

With proper preparation, it's said to taste like a great big rabbit.

When making Crazy Simple Marinara sauce, we simmer an onion in the sauce for an hour then throw it away. No joke. No woodchucks.

Chapter 10.1 Crazy Simple Marinara Sauce

Serves 6 to 8 Preparation: 5 minutes Cooking: 1 hour 30 minutes.

Don't be fooled by the simplicity of this recipe. The results are legend!

Ingredients:

- 28 ounce can of whole peeled tomatoes.
- 1 medium (baseball sized) yellow onion
- 4 tablespoons of butter

Lets get cooking.

o   Cut onion in half, peel outer layers.

o   In a 4 quart stock pot place onion halves, 4 tablespoons of butter and 28 ounces of canned tomatoes.

o   Simmer on low heat. Crush tomatoes every 15 minutes in the pot. After one hour, remove the onion halves

o   Simmer for another half hour, stirring and crushing.

Your tomato sauce is done. Simple, humble and delicious. Taste it. If you think it needs more salt, add a pinch.

Chapter 11. How to Bread and Fry Poultry

There is more than one way to skin a pheasant, swing a cat, or cook up those delicious, tender pheasant filets. Let's use the frying pan.

Things to know/ why this works

Once the details of breading and frying are understood, it's easy to apply to any fowl.

Served over pasta, Pheasant Milanese features a fried breaded filet seasoned with oregano and basil. An American Southern Style dish would have a white gravy, cornbread and turnip greens. I'll be damned before I publish a recipe called "Chicken Fried Pheasant", but the techniques used would be the same.

Pheasant filets are thin and cook quickly. On the other hand, thick chicken filets must be pounded thin with a meat mallet.

Getting the breading to stick is the first order of business.

This recipe uses Panko, a Japanese light and flaky breadcrumb that stores in the cupboard for a long time. It crisps well and has a mild flavor. Pheasant, oregano, basil and black pepper are the stars of the show.

Dry the filet with paper towels, then drag them through a little pile of flour or cornstarch seasoned with salt and pepper.

Shake all the loose flour off, then dip into a bowl with a beaten egg. Coat it well, rub a bit with eggy fingers if needed!

Next, dredge the wet filet through spiced Panko bread crumbs, pressing them in. Let the result rest in the refrigerator for ten minutes. This is part of getting the bread crumbs to set firmly before frying.

The process will take up kitchen real-estate. Clearing clutter and planning ahead will pay dividends. You'll need a place to pat the filet dry, and space for the foot long piece of waxed paper that holds a flower mixture. A small bowl with beaten egg sits next to another bit of waxed paper heaped with breadcrumb and spices. Use a plate or cooking rack to hold the expertly breaded filets before they go into the 'fridge.

Next, fry the cutlets in a *very hot* pan of oil.

Use a 9 inch non-stick **frying pan** with smooth, rounded inner corners. The frying oils and juices swirl and flow better with this design. A pan with sharp, square inner corners is called a sauté pan. It works almost as well.

Extra virgin olive oil alone might taste heavy, so dilute it with lighter vegetable oil. Both have a high smoke-point.

Greasy filets result from cooking too cool. But overheated oil breaks down into bluish smoke, short-chain degradation products, polar compounds, and free-fatty acids. Not only will this taste bad, but might give Chinese Military Cooks cancer over time, according to a longitudinal study. *It's on the internet.*

Without a thermal imaging camera in your kitchen, how are you supposed to know how to "fry between 360 and 375° Fahrenheit, and never below 325°"?

Heat the pan slowly until the oil is shimmering hot, not quite smoking, with only the faintest hint of smoke wisps beginning to rise. Then slide food into the pan. This will cool the oil, so turn up the heat briefly.

Overcooking is all too easy. Three to four minutes per side is enough.

Separate small 'tenders' might take two minutes and thirty seconds per side, while an enormous filet might take four minutes before flipping.

Use a spoon to drizzle hot oil over the top as the breaded meat cooks. When the edges are golden brown, flip and continue basting.

When the 'poke test' reveals a firmness about the same as pressing the tip of your nose, the filets are done. The FDA says the internal temperature must be 165° F. With experience, confidence in the poke test will grow. It's hard to use a meat thermometer on a skinny filet on a smokin' hot fry pan.

Drain excess oil from the hot breaded filets by resting them on a cooling rack or plate with paper towels for two minutes. Place the breaded filet on a bed of fresh pasta, then ladle a healthy diagonal stripe of premium red pasta sauce across it.

Served with fresh bread and a nice Cabernet Sauvignon or Zinfandel, sparkling water or lemonade, you've got a perfect meal.

Notes

Pheasant Milanese. Breaded and fried, over fresh ravioli with red sauce and mixed veggies

Chapter 11.1 Recipe: Pheasant Milanese.

Serves: 2 Preparation: 10 minutes Cooking: 6-7 minutes

Breaded and fried. Served with red sauce over pasta. Pasta sauce is simmered and pasta is made per directions on the package while the pheasant breasts cool in the refrigerator to secure their breading.

Ingredients

- 2 pheasant breast filets
- 3 tablespoons all purpose flour or cornstarch
- 1 egg
- 1/3 cup Panko bread crumbs
- 2 tablespoons Turkish oregano
- 2 teaspoons dried basil
- 1 teaspoon dried parsley (for color)
- ¼ teaspoon salt
- 1 teaspoon fresh ground black pepper
- 2 tablespoons Extra-virgin olive oil
- 1 tablespoon vegetable oil

For the side dishes

- 9 ounces fresh fettucine
- 24 ounces premium pasta sauce
- 1 baguette

Lets get cooking.

- Mix 3 tablespoons flour with ¼ teaspoon salt and ½ teaspoon ground black pepper.

- Separately, mix 1/3 cup Panko, 2 tablespoons Turkish oregano, 2 teaspoons basil, 1 teaspoon parsley, ½ teaspoon black pepper.

- Dry pheasant breast filets, dredge in flour mixture. Coat filets with beaten egg.

- Dredge and heavily coat the wet filet with Panko mixture. Set aside in refrigerator for ten minutes.

- Bring 2 tablespoons Extra-virgin olive oil and 1 tablespoon vegetable oil to high heat- 375° F. Oil should be shimmering hot, the faintest hints of smoke beginning.

- Fry breaded filets. Maintain temperature below the smoke point and above 325°. Cook for 3 minutes. Edges of breading should be browned.

- Flip the filets. Fry for 3 minutes. Test for completion. Remove to cooling rack or plate lined with paper towels to drain.

Plate a golden brown breaded pheasant filet over a nest of fresh pasta. Ladle a healthy serving of red pasta sauce in an artistic diagonal across the breast. Add a few slices of French bread, and serve.

Chapter 12.1 Recipe: Pheasant Francese.

Serves: 4 Preparation: 20 minutes Cooking: 25 minutes

Baked with lemon and white wine. Served over pasta. Don't limit yourself to grilling or frying; poaching is another great way to cook pheasant. With the addition of this bold and zesty lemon sauce, the pasta takes on a refreshing and lively taste.

Pheasant Francese—poached and baked with a zingy lemon and white wine sauce–why not make things interesting and opt for spinach linguine or fettuccine?

Choose good ingredients: real lemons for slices and juice, extra virgin olive oil, Parmesan cheese and fresh spices. Dry parsley will help absorb some moisture and add color. While two percent milk will do, half-and-half provides a richer flavor.

Recommended white wine for cooking should be of the quality you'd serve to guests. Sauvignon Blanc or Pinot Grigio are top choices. Consider a dry Riesling to bring out some interesting flavors, or try an unoaked Chardonnay to add richness. For those who enjoy the taste of Chablis, it can help balance out the lemony flavor of the dish. The tart lemon will perfectly complement the earthy flavor of a steamed and buttered asparagus side dish.

Ingredients

- 4 boneless pheasant breast filets
- 1 cup dry white wine
- 1 cup whole milk
- 1 cup Panko breadcrumbs
- 1 cup Parmesan cheese, grated
- 1 lemon for 4 thin slices and to produce ¼ cup juice
- 1 cup low sodium chicken broth
- 2 tablespoons dried parsley
- ½ cup olive oil
- ¼ teaspoon salt
- ½ teaspoon pepper
- 18 ounces fresh pasta or 1 pound dried artisanal pasta.

Lets get cooking.

- Soak chicken in milk for about 10 minutes.
- Preheat oven to 350° F.
- Mix breadcrumbs, Parmesan cheese, and dried parsley. Make sure each slice is well-covered by dredging each slice of pheasant in this mixture. Refrigerate for 10 minutes.
- Bring olive oil to shimmering heat in a large skillet. Quickly braise pheasant breasts on both sides until lightly browned, about 90 seconds. Do not overcook.
- Place breasts in a greased, uncovered baking dish. Lightly salt and pepper with one slice of lemon on top of each piece.
- Remove excess oil from the skillet but leave 1 tablespoon of oil and the residue from brazing.
- Add white wine, lemon juice, and chicken broth to skillet. Reduce liquid by half, then pour over the pheasant.
- Bake at 350° F for 20-25 minutes or until the liquid bubbles.

Serve over fresh pasta with a side of steamed asparagus. Drizzle delicious juices from the baking dish over the filet. If you haven't tried this style of Italian cooking, you're in for a treat.

Chapter 13. Brand-New Things

The fox-red Labrador wagged his tail as hard as a tail can be wagged. Havoc jumped from the back of the car and capered to burn off excitement. He sprinted crazy-dog circles in the fresh snow. The familiar hunting land was strange today.

His owner left ankle deep tracks away from the car as he thumbed three shells into his brand new Fabarms L4s shotgun. The two expected a big loop through marshy hunting grounds along the stream, but they kept to the white, windswept tractor trail. The snow was less deep than in the swale. That's what you call the land off to the side.

Transformed into a winter faerie land, familiar fields lay below yesterday's winter storm. Somewhere out there, pheasants were hiding. The dog was exploring a clean white slate, free of crisscrossing tracks or complex layered scents. Only recent snowfall clinging in the tree branches could grace nature with such profound beauty and stillness.

They walked and walked, making the first boot or paw prints on the powdery trail. The dog found a spot that smelled faintly promising, but search as he might, he found no bird to make fly. Fluffy snow clung and twinkled along tree branches, ice glistened at the shore of the creek. Fresh rabbit, squirrel and mouse trails were crisp in the new snowfall, but no large, splay-toed pheasant tracks. The dog ignored the chickadees and blackbirds, but the man enjoyed their company.

It had taken the steam from both their gaits, hiking three miles in six inches of snow. Trudging beside the pond, the old man could only think of setting one heavy boot ahead of the other, counting footfalls. He started over again at every hundred steps. With the sun setting and temperature dropping, he was cold and clammy. His lower back hurt, and the shotgun weighed on his arm.

Their loop hiked, the car was close at hand, and it was time to go home. The dog trotted at heel, too fatigued to bound ahead. To their right, the pond had recently iced over. It was not thick enough to support a man, and perhaps not a dog. The snow seemed darker near the middle. Havoc cocked his ears as he took a few steps towards the flat white expanse, curious about the state of his summer swimming hole. The man whistled him back. Disagreeable adventure with a wet and muddy dog flashed through his mind. He was cold.

The Lab dropped his nose to the snow, sniffed, then waved his tail stiffly at top speed. That was "bird tail", and always meant a pheasant was nearby. Nose in the snow, tail flagging, he rushed along a fresh scent, charging a winding path with obsession. The man jogged through the drifts after him, all fatigue forgotten.

Bounding into the woods, chest deep in drifted snow, the flushing-retriever sprang like a small red deer. He bounced back and forth among the trees, seeking the bird. His nose told him it was close, and he was growing closer.

A ring-necked bird erupted in an explosion of beating wings, cackling from its hiding place blanketed in snow. Shocking bright colors of golden yellow, red, green, and brown, the bird bumped into a scruffy poplar tree as he flushed. Tiny piles of white showered down. More blobs fell as the bird flapped, blundered and cackled to break free of the branches.

Knee deep in a drift, the sudden ruckus caught the hunter off guard. He jerked in surprise, all attention on the bird flapping clumsily, too close for a shot. Congratulating himself on his restraint, he watched it over the bead of his shotgun. He had shot a tree in a situation like this two years ago.

The bird rocketed from the branches and flew over the man, so close it seemed he could have struck it with an outstretched barrel. Excitement got the better of him. He fired too soon, too close, and missed.

Twisting, feet stuck in deep snow, he followed the flight of the bird with his gun. He tugged at the fore-end to cycle a new shell into the chamber. He gauged the edge of the pond with his peripheral vision. Absolutely nothing would prevent that dog from retrieving, so he considered the thin ice carefully. But something was wrong. The forearm would not pull back, he could not reload.

He tugged and tugged at the fore-end of his shotgun. Reloading had meant pulling his front hand back and forth for years. It had become a reflex, like snapping the safety off, or covering his nose for a sneeze. The large golden bird got smaller and smaller in the distance.

A sudden realization dawned on the frustrated hunter. He wasn't holding his 1946 Ithaca Model 37 pump-action shotgun. This was his brand new Italian semi-automatic. He could have simply pulled the trigger again. So there he was, feet stuck in deep snow, hips squared towards a tree, and upper body twisted as far to the right as possible. The only pheasant of the day was even farther to the right, and growing smaller in the distance.

With a grunt, he twisted more and pulled the trigger. Perhaps it was just to hear the gun boom in frustration, because the bird was out of range. As if in slow motion, he lost his balance and sat, wet and cold, in the deep snow.

"God damn it." These were the only words he had spoken since breakfast.

The bird flew across the edge of the pond, with a red rocket dog skimming beneath him, graceful as any winter wolf after prey on a nature show. Havoc returned with his best grin. White teeth, happy red tongue lolling, expressive brown eyes and perked up floppy ears. He was a domestic Labrador again, wondering why no bird had fallen.

The hunter shook his head and rose from the cold and wet. One hand was warm in a mitten, but his trigger hand was bare and red. If dogs could talk, hunters would gather less often. The man struggled to stand, and Havoc gave him a wet, unwanted lick on the face.

Despite the annoying demonstration of love, the hunter gave out biscuits from his pocket.

The walk back to their small four-wheel-drive vehicle took twice as long as when he'd begun with fresh legs. He felt defeated, skunked by the fancy new gun. As his body warmed on the drive home, he considered the contented dog sleeping in the back, and that dinner would be waiting.

His wife would ask if they had any luck.

Sometimes the pheasant wins, Yes, they had luck, it could not have been a more beautiful winter day.

And the dog wasn't talking.

Chapter 14. Thawing Frozen Poultry

When luck doesn't favor the hunter for a while, it's time to pull legs or carcass from the freezer. The best way to thaw frozen poultry is–don't.

When possible, put frozen pheasant, straight into steaming sauce to simmer or boiling water for soup. Frozen meat will cool the sauce, so the pan needs a little turbo boost of heat to get back to simmering. For soup, the old saying is 'soup boiled is soup spoiled.'

If a recipe calls for simmering, adjust time upwards by fifteen minutes for frozen meat.

According to the US Department of Agriculture, 40° F to 140° F is the bacteria "Danger Zone". It's Thawing pheasant meat below the danger zone will take twenty-four hours in the refrigerator. It will be safe in the 'fridge for 3-5 days. In a hurry and can't wait twenty-four hours? Place a Ziploc bag of frozen meat in a large bowl and run **cold water** over it. In about twenty minutes, it will thaw four frozen legs enough to pull from each other. Plunk partly frozen legs in steaming hot, lightly boiling sauce.

Defrosting with **cold water** keeps outer layers out of the danger zone while the inner core is defrosting at a faster rate. Warm water is what bacteria love.

Once thawed, frozen meat becomes susceptible to bacterial growth and must be cooked soon. Meat that is frozen twice will experience cellular damage and loss of moisture. Re-freezing won't destroy the bacteria, which has grown in number while unfrozen. Although there are certain circumstances where meat can be refrozen safely, it will always result in a significant loss of quality.

Freezing cuts of pheasant separately by breast, legs, and carcass/giblets ensures you can easily access the portions you need for meals. Cook each cut of meat differently.

Chapter 15. A Feast: Pheasant Neapolitan with Mixed Vegetables

Pheasant legs simmered in pasta sauce. Pheasant Neapolitan is elegant, fabulous, and only a peanut butter sandwich is easier to make. Though it's presented for two, this meal would scale up for a brilliant dinner party.

Things to know/ why this works

Simmering for two hours is okay. Three hours is good, but after four hours the meat and small bones might float free and create a minefield for eating. Don't overdo a good thing.

Use high-quality ingredients: premium pasta sauce, fresh pasta and bread, and colorful vegetables.

The first two legs will simmer in twenty-four ounces of pasta sauce. Four legs would simmer in thirty-six ounces, and six in about forty-eight ounces of sauce.

Cooking with bacon is cheating, but let's do it often. Wild game is very lean, bacon brings needed fat and salty seasoning. Cut the bacon into 1/8 pound chunks, freeze the rest for future cooking. It's a man-cooking staple.

There will be plenty of tomato sauce to mop up with bread, so get a fresh French baguette or loaf of Italian bread. Ciabatta, Coppia Ferrarese, or Pane Toscano are good choices.

Red table wine, Chianti, Merlot, Shiraz, Zinfandel, are all perfect for this meal. Even a fresh Pino Grigio white wine works for those who won't drink red.

Non-alcoholic drinks with acidity and flavor complement the hearty, sweet pheasant and rich tomato sauce. Sparkling water can vary from bubbly mineral water to San Pellegrino flavors. Coca-cola or Izze sparkling juices are also interesting choices.

As a side dish, we'll have a frozen mix of colorful carrots, green beans, sweet peas, corn and dreaded lima beans.

The kaleidoscopic combination adds a splash of whimsy, while butter over the top adds ~~guilt~~ flavor. Steamed, sauteed, or roasted; It's easy and fun. While the microwave is easy, consider a new way to cook these veggies!

Notes

Chapter 15.1 Recipe: Pheasant Neapolitan

Serves: 2 Preparation: 10 minutes Cooking: 3 to 4 hours

Simmered in tomato sauce, served over pasta. Deceptively simple, the only trick is a long simmer in great sauce!

Ingredients:

- 2 pheasant legs (thigh and drumstick).
- 9 oz. **Fresh pasta:** linguine, fettuccine, or ravioli.
- One 24 ounce jar of pasta sauce for first two legs, 12 ounces per pair afterwards.
- 3 slices of bacon per pair of legs, chopped. Because bacon.
- 1 tablespoon olive oil.

Don't forget:

- Fresh bread. French baguette, Ciabatta, Coppia Ferrarese, or Pane Toscano.

Lets get cooking.

- Chop the bacon into 3/8 inch squares. In a 9 1/2 inch skillet (with lid), fry bacon at medium low heat with 1 tablespoon olive oil for 5 minutes. Render the bacon fat to clear color. Do not overheat, the pan should not smoke.

- Turn stove heat to medium-high. Sear raw pheasant legs in the oil and bacon for two minutes per side. The legs should be light gray with hints of brown. Add tomato sauce, cover.

- Alternative for frozen pheasant legs: Cook bacon in pan, then add sauce and bring to a light boil, add frozen legs. Ladle hot sauce over legs. Cover pan.

- Reduce heat to simmer for 3-4 hours. The pan should barely bubble. Fold steaming hot sauce over the legs every half hour.

Remove a pheasant leg, plate it over a bed of pasta and ladle sauce over the top.

Set side plates for guests to discard small bones. The meal must be eaten carefully, watching for inedibles and the rare instance of lost shot. But the meat is easily picked clean with a fork.

It's hard to imagine that some hunters don't eat the legs. Inconceivable!

Cooking snobs might sneer at mixed frozen vegetables, but pheasant season begins in late September. Fresh local produce isn't available. Checkmate!

Chapter 15.2 Recipe: Mixed Frozen Veggies.

Serves 4. Preparation: 2 minutes Cooking: 5-25 minutes.

Steamed, Sauteed, or Baked. The simple bag of frozen veggies from the supermarket is a bright splash of color and can be prepared in many ways.

Ingredients:

- 10 oz frozen mixed vegetables: Carrots, green beans, corn, peas.
- 1 tablespoon butter
- 1 tablespoon olive oil (sauteed or baked option)
- 1 pinch garlic salt (sauteed or baked option)
- 1 sprinkling dried red pepper flakes (sauteed or baked option)

Lets get cooking.

Microwave.

Toss frozen mixed vegetables into a casserole dish, then the microwave oven. Follow instructions on the bag. Put a tablespoon of butter over the top and serve. Good, but we can do better.

Sauteed.

We can sauté the mixed veggies in a frying pan, right from the freezer. Bring one tablespoon of butter and one tablespoon of olive oil to lightly smoking. Add veggies. Medium high heat, for 5-7 minutes. Consider adding a pinch of garlic salt and a sprinkling of dried red pepper flakes.

Roasted.

To roast frozen veggies in the oven. Coat a rimmed cookie sheet with olive oil. Bring the pan to 425° F in the oven.

Lightly coat frozen veggies in 1 Tablespoon of olive oil and a small pinch of garlic salt. Spread them evenly on the hot pan. Cook for 20-25 minutes. Flip them halfway through the roasting time. Dried red pepper flakes are an option.

Chapter 16. A Feast: Pheasant Marsala, Parsley Rice and Sauteed Green Beans

Pheasant Marsala is involved cooking. Mushrooms, wine, butter, bacon, olive oil and cream, combined to make your own delicious sauce for the legs from three pheasants.

Be prepared for sticker shock: a box of premium shotgun shells costs less than what you'll pay for these ingredients. But you'll know the satisfaction of creating a sophisticated wine reduction. Mushrooms cook down and thicken to a creamy sophisticated sauce with unique mouth feel. You managed to shoot three pheasants, you can do this.

My friend Stewart baked his first lasagna. It smelled fabulous. Darned good for his first attempt. Soon, everyone was politely spitting out olive pits. Stuart smacked his head. He used unpitted olives, a mistake. The lasagna was fine. It was delicious, charming and amusing. He did better the next time.

Another good friend, Jason, made garlic bread. He mistook 'heads' of garlic for 'cloves'. He was learning to cook. We washed his delicious buttery powerhouse down with good beer, and wives quarantined husbands to the couch for the next day or so. It was worth it.

Have courage. Pheasant Marsala is hotshot cooking, but you can do it. It's delicious, leftovers are fantastic, and sometimes a hankering for white wine and mushroom sauce tugs at your taste buds. What could go wrong? Nothing serious.

Things to know/ why this works

Our pheasant with mushroom sauce tastes good, and simmering is the way to cook legs, but this recipe presents a lot of brown color. White Basmati rice and vibrant sauteed green beans provide vibrant color variation and taste great. If you want to use another rice, it's an easy substitution.

Instead of using Marsala wine, this recipe uses Chardonnay. Chardonnay is good for cooking and the cook, who would much rather sip leftovers while waiting for things to simmer.

Some say alcohol cooks completely out of wine sauce, but there is some debate. Those who don't want such beverages in the home can replace one cup of white wine with 1/2 cup chicken broth and 1/2 cup apple cider vinegar. Or they replace one cup of white wine with chicken broth and white wine vinegar. All variations taste good.

This recipe uses lots of mushrooms. They reduce for this sauce and contribute to rich flavor layering. At a minimum, buy eight ounces of Shiitake mushrooms, then more varieties, as fancy as your wallet allows, to about 25-30 ounces total.

Shiitake mushrooms have a rich, savory flavor. It's a perfect example of 'umami'. Parmesan cheese, Japanese seaweed, or oysters are examples of this flavor category. Cut off the woody stems before slicing Shitake mushrooms.

Porcini mushrooms are nutty, earthy, and add a nice brown color to the sauce. Get some.

Crimini are young Portobello mushrooms. They have a rich, earthy, almost beefy taste. Break off the stem before chopping them up. Lobster mushrooms are sweet and nutty. Chantarelles are sweet with a hint of apricot or peach. If you can't find Lobster mushrooms, try Chantarelles.

White Button mushrooms are the common supermarket ones. They have a mild, earthy flavor that increases with cooking. They taste good, and are the least expensive.

Cooking the mushrooms changes their flavor. Flavors will layer in complexity when we add the mushrooms in two stages. We don't dump all the ingredients in a pot. That's deer camp cooking.

The cooking vessel must hold a large volume of mushrooms, withstand searing heat, then distribute that heat evenly for a long simmer on the stove top. This recipe calls for a Dutch oven, a big cooking pot made of heavy enameled steel, with a massive thick lid. In France, it's called a 'cocotte', in the Netherlands they call it a braadpaan.

A big frying pan, a crock pot, ingenuity and extra clean-up can replace a Dutch oven.

Unsalted butter and low sodium chicken broth are fine choices. Guests can always add salt to their preference, but they can not remove what you've put in.

Drink options: Chardonnay, Chenin Blanc or Sauvignon Blanc. Champaign, Cider (with or without alcohol), or sparkling water.

They'll know you busted your chops to create something special for dinner.

Chapter 16.1 Pheasant Marsala

Serves: 6 Preparation: 30 minutes Cooking: 2.5 hours

Pheasant leg simmered in white wine and mushrooms. Mushrooms, onion, bacon, cream and wine reduce to deep brown sauce with smooth and savory flavors that complement wild game.

A Dutch oven can be replaced with a large covered cast iron frying pan or skillet and crock pot.

Ingredients:

- 6 whole skinned/ de-tendoned pheasant legs
- ¼ pound bacon, chopped
- 4 tablespoons butter (unsalted)
- 2 tablespoons olive oil
- ½ yellow onion, diced
- 3 or 4 cloves garlic, minced
- Mushrooms. 20-30 ounces, mixed, consisting of:

  5 ounces Shiitake mushrooms, chopped

  1 pint Crimini or White Button mushrooms, sliced or chopped

  5 ounces Lobster or Chanterelle mushrooms chopped or sliced

  5 ounces Porcini Mushrooms, chopped
- 1 cup Chardonnay
- 1 cup chicken broth (low sodium)
- ¼ cup heavy cream
- ½ cup fresh parsley, chopped
- 3 tablespoons cornstarch
- 2 teaspoons ground black pepper

- Remove tough stems from mushrooms, depending on variety. Chop to bite sized morsels, 1/8 inch thick. That's the thickness of two US quarters, or 3 mm.
- Chop 1/4 cup parsley, fine.
- Chop 1/2 yellow onion, coarse. Preheat Dutch oven to medium high, with 2 Tablespoons butter, 1 Tablespoon olive oil.

- Cook 1/8 pound chopped bacon. Do not overheat. Bacon fat should be clear. (5 minutes.)
- Sear pheasant legs in hot oil and bacon fat, one minute per side, then set them away. Color should be gray, with faint brown overtones.
- Caramelize 1/2 chopped yellow onion and 3 minced cloves of garlic. Onion color should vary from clear to light brownish
- Deglaze the pot with a healthy splash (3 tablespoons) of Chardonnay wine. Use a wooden spoon to get all the flavorful stuff at the bottom of the pan free.

- Add 2/3 of the mushrooms. Cover, cook for 5 minutes, stirring occasionally.

- Add 1 cup white wine. Set heat to high, until the wine is reduced in volume by half. Then reduce heat to simmer.

- Add pheasant legs and 1 cup chicken broth. Simmer for 2 hours, covered.

- Add remaining mushrooms. Simmer 20 minutes. Layering the time adds depth to flavor and texture.

- Thicken the sauce. Mix three tablespoons of corn starch with three tablespoons of water in a cup. Bring the mushroom sauce to a light boil. Stir splashes of cornstarch slurry into sauce slowly, stirring thoroughly to prevent clumping.

Turn off heat. Slowly stir in cream and 2 tablespoons of butter.

Allow to sit covered for 5-15 minutes. Pheasant Marsala can warm while the rest of the meal is prepared for plating. Stir in ¼ cup chopped parsley, two minutes before serving

Tender Pheasant Legs in White Wine and Mushroom Reduction

Chapter 16.2 Recipe: Parsley Rice

Serves: 6 Preparation 5 minutes. Cooking: 12 minutes

The parsley is here to make pretty green flecks, but it's a nice touch! Parsley can be fresh or dried.

Ingredients

- Rice:
- 2 Cups Basmati rice
- 1/4 Cup parsley, finely chopped
- 2 Tablespoons butter

Lets get cooking.

- Prepare rice per the directions on the package.
- Stir 1/4 cup of finely chopped parsley and 2 tablespoons of butter into the pot of cooked rice.
- Wait one minute. Serve.

Chapter 16.3 Recipe: Sauteed Green Beans

Serves: 6 Preparation: 5 minutes Cooking: 5 minutes

Green beans and salted cashews, flash fried. Yum. Note: a Planters Nuts snack bag of cashews is perfect, in case you don't want to eat most of the whole can of cashews all by yourself on the drive home from the store.

Ingredients:

- 1 1/2 pound green beans, cleaned with the ends nipped off.
- 1 tablespoon olive oil
- ½ tablespoon butter
- ½ teaspoon crushed red pepper flakes
- 2 tablespoons chopped, lightly salted roasted cashews.

Lets get Cooking.

o Bring 1 inch of water in a 9 inch frying pan to a boil. Blanch (that means boil) green beans for two minutes, then run them under cold water in a colander. Drain.

o Dry skillet and bring it and olive oil to high heat, making sure the pan is well coated. Then add butter and crushed red pepper flakes.

o Stir-fry blanched green beans for 2 minutes in the very hot pan.

o Reduce heat, add chopped cashews, toss in pan for 30 seconds. Remove from heat to serving dish.

Stir in 1/4 cup of fresh chopped parsley. Delicious vibrant green beans, with cashews!

Chapter 17: Preserve Hunting

"How can I adjust my home defense shotgun to shoot skeet and hunt pheasants?" Andy posted this question on a popular shotgun chat board.

My answer to that chat-board question was so complicated that I looked up his profile instead. He lived nearby.

This was back at the end of the 2019-2022 COVID pandemic. Sensible people were getting out of the house again, gathering in public, and socializing after two years of isolation. We agreed to rendezvous at my trap and skeet club in late January. We still wore our N-95 respirator masks, although the clubhouse was empty.

We found our kids were about the same age, his son a Junior in college, while my daughter had just graduated. We had much in common and hit it right off. Andy was retiring from work, while I had beaten him to that prize by a few years. He wanted to learn how to pheasant hunt.

"My wife thought it would be good for me to get a shotgun," he said. "I've had a romantic notion of going hunting, but it's not a family tradition. I'm starting from scratch."

"Same for me, just a few years ago. My father grew up in northern Pennsylvania, trout fishing, and hunting grouse or deer. We moved to the Midwest when I was a kid, but we never hunted pheasants. He taught me to fly fish for bluegills off a pier, though."

"Those rascals put up a fight. I'd rather fly fish from a pier, too." Andy's eyes lit up. As I said, we had a lot in common.

We uncased his black Mossberg shotgun, triple checked it was unloaded, then I observed his stance and swing in the lounge. We extended the telescoping combat-style stock as far as it would reach. I scratched my head. He had no place to rest his cheek on that stock tube.

"Andy, this won't work. For wing shooting, you weld your cheek to the stock. When you snug the gun to your shoulder, a proper fit will set your eye to the same place, every time. The gun shoots where you look."

Andy moved his head back and forth, then turned his head sideways. Even with an unnatural stretch, he couldn't get his cheek on the black steel tube.

"This is not comfortable at all."

"Your shotgun is set up for combat games. We could make it work for deer or turkey, but it'll never work for bird hunting." I delivered the bad news with a sigh.

"Excellent. I need to buy a new shotgun!" His eyes flickered to the blued steel and walnut Italian gun I had set aside. I saw a gleam in his eye and a grin spread across his face.

I'm stout and barrel-chested, five-foot six inches tall. Andy is five foot ten, thin, with an athletic build. I knew it would be too short when I handed him my favorite shotgun, but short as it was, mine had a longer length-of-pull than his.

My beautiful wood stock was checkered and designed for hitting targets in flight. His eyes opened wide as he hefted the gun. "Whoa! This is a couple of pounds lighter than mine." Then he shouldered and swept his aim across the empty room. "It's completely different."

I had brought shims, pads and masking tape, anticipating a stock fitting session. We adjusted his stance, how far apart to set his feet, where to point his toes, slight forward lean. Then I repeated the crazy phrase my skeet coach shared twenty-five years earlier,

"You aim a shotgun with your hips."

"You just said to aim by looking at the target."

"That, too." We adjusted his feet and angle of his hips. "Set them to where you'll shoot, not where you begin the swing. Notice the difference?"

"Ohhhhh."

We kept taping thin plastic shims to the stock, creeping up on elegance until we found what we were looking for. With these temporary dimensions, every time Andy drew the stock to his shoulder, his eyes pointed right down the barrel. I wrote the dimensions on a slip of paper. They looked familiar.

"It seems we shimmed my 'compact' gun stock back to the original dimensions of a 'standard' L4s. You're close to their idea of the average man."

"I want one." Andy reluctantly gave my gun back. The shims, padding and masking tape, had done their job. He was going to tell his wife he needed a new shotgun, and he'd join a shooting club closer to his home.

I got a hearty handshake. Although I wasn't an expert stock fitter, I was better than a sales associate at the big-box store. We got his measurements and I had given my new friend the best advice for any shooter—join a club, get a shotgun that fits, and bust fifty clay pigeons with a coach.

A few weeks later I got a text message:

Hey! Let's meet at my club and hunt! The club's dog handler is out of town for a few weeks. Bring Havoc!

My dog Havoc had met Andy when we were discussing shotgun fitting. He thought my new friend was fine and appreciated a man who gave out biscuits quickly.

We would love it. I've never been on a preserve hunt, I texted back.

Great! You bring the dog, I'll pay for the birds. Renting a dog and handler is expensive.

Renting a dog? I was gobsmacked. Having your own dog is two-thirds of bird hunting.

I was curious to experience this aspect of hunting, but worried Havoc might embarrass me. The game preserve sounded fancy, while my young Labrador and I hunt in the rough. That terrain is perfect for a Flushing Retriever like him, but preserve hunting belongs to the aristocratic Pointers. So I thought.

Hunting after season is legal at private clubs. Andy scheduled one more hunt for late March. There were unfamiliar elements, like scheduling a time to hunt, planted birds, employees, and a restaurant on site. I was determined to keep an open mind and prayed Havoc wouldn't embarrass me.

For the dog, the air around the Lodge parking lot must have been an olfactory explosion. His nose told him there were pheasants. Lots of them, maybe millions. He dragged me at the end of his leash to go see. Passing a tall green hedge, he stood stock still. His eyes bugged out, then he gave a little whine.

Hundreds of ring-necks stared back at him from behind a black netted fence fifty yards away. An enormous bird farm was on the other side of the parking lot.

His tail grew stiff and wagged quick. He looked up at me. I could read his mind.

Look! Look! Birds! So many birds. We could... you could... I found BIRDS! The Labrador's eyes sparkled. He wore a wide grin with white teeth and a pink lolling tongue.

"Yes, those are birds, but they are not for us. Let's go play with the ball." I pulled his favorite blue latex sphere from my pocket.

His eyes lit up. *Ball! Almost as good as birds.*

The well-maintained grounds included a large grassy field perfect for a dog to chase a blue bouncing ball. The excitement of 300 bold pheasants had charged his system with adrenaline. I whipped the thing fifty or sixty yards with his flinger. He chased after it like a rocket. We met a lot of men with seriously trained dogs, a few cute puppies, and two young boys who came over to give Havoc proper thumps on the chest.

The boys scratched Havoc behind his ears as they waited for their dad and grandpa to get organized for a three generation hunt. Andy turned up, beaming a smile.

He had set an appointment, and a game keeper had hidden six pheasants about the Northside West designated area, about a mile away. It was a well-organized operation, and here we stood on a beautiful day. Our last hunt, post season.

Even though staff had planted the birds, it wasn't as easy as I thought. It took some time to get in sync, and a few birds escaped because I forgot we should shoot hens. Andy had to learn Havoc's body language, too.

A lot of work in squishy lowland silt loam produced our first bird, tucked behind my field jacket.

We ventured into standing water more than ankle deep up our Wellies. No one fell down or found a hole deeper than the top of their boot, a major triumph. Then we strategically sandbagged, pretending to adjust jackets and guns, while actually watching distant hunters at the edge of the neighboring field. As if on cue, they flushed a bird.

A fair bit of shooting followed as their quarry flew away unharmed. Eventually, it landed in our reserved field. We had chased one of our pheasants to their area earlier, with equally ineffective noise. It seemed a fair trade.

We made our way to the distant spot the bonus pheasant had landed. These birds can run fast and often go great distances after landing. We had to hunt for it, but we had a Labrador with a good nose.

Andy shot well. I need not have worried about Havoc, he was adapting to this new style perfectly. Two birds in the bag.

The three of us climbed up a hill into the sun, and dry open fields. We got to talking about how our kids were doing, their new jobs, shotgun shells, and home remodeling.

A hen flushed, and I shot a difficult fast-crossing approach. Now three birds were ours.
We walked in the sunshine on higher ground atop the hill, which made for easier footing. Havoc put nose to ground. By now, Andy knew the signs and had his gun ready. The dog worked the field as we followed. That bird held tight until a Labrador nose pushed deep into its hiding place.

Cackling, the golden bird flushed, then swerved. It showed vibrant green and red head, the white ring around his neck, and long brown striped tail feathers as it curved away. It presented a tough shot.

Andy drew his L4s to shoulder and fired instinctively. BOOM. The bird went down onto the tractor trail, forty paces ahead, stone dead. Havoc had him in a flash. No chance of losing this one. The dog retrieved at a gallop, ears flapping.

My ears burned, so happy for my friend. He had a Zen moment, and I was there to see it. That was a hard shot and my dog was hunting for him. It all came together.

"Great shooting."

"I don't even remember aiming," he admitted with a sheepish grin. With a pheasant in his hand, it was easy to keep Havoc close for a few photos. "We have four birds, and the sun is going down. Does the dog need a bath?"

Havoc's eyebrows raised. He recognized the word. *Bath.* He was half covered in dried black mud and smelled like a swamp.

The Lodge was a reminder that the society of hunting men is unique. The Pro Shop was posh. The restaurant looked warm, and the bar looked comfortable, all in natural wood grains and log cabin construction. Middle class to wealthy men were all dirty and rumpled, everyone in their stocking feet.

The sign outside the bar was clear: "No muddy boots in the bar or restaurant!" A wide selection of muck covered Wellingtons rested in the big plastic tray below the sign.

The bird cleaning room and dog shower were heaven for man and beast. They dedicated a room with stainless steel counters for hunters to butcher their catch. Andy traded his fresh game and four dollars for two neatly packaged, already prepared pheasants. That's a bargain.
The shower room had a waist high stall with hand-held sprayer, for the exclusive use of canines. Warm water and baby shampoo had rinsed dark black mud from the coat, paws and tail of a room full of clean Pointers, Retrievers and Flushing dogs. They ran about without collars, wagging tails and sniffing all the important places. Even a bath could not spoil the gathering.

Havoc slept soundly on the drive home, shiny clean and smelling of Johnson & Johnson.

Next fall, I'll be showing my friend the hunting grounds near where we live. The terrain is rougher, and we might go miles without seeing a bird. We might bag our limit or return empty-handed. I can show him the rocky bottom section of the creek where we get mud off the dogs. On the way home, we can stop at the fast-food joint for coffee and a cheeseburger.

The preserve hunt club has a lot going for it. I learned the birds were smaller than their cousins in the wilds, and their first wobbly flight might very well be their last. The breast filets were smaller, and hens were even smaller than the cocks. With two men hunting side by side, I could see that we might have been over-gunned with an ounce and a quarter of lead shot each. But it was a great experience and I'm grateful for it.

My friend Andy called a breeder about a puppy, he's getting a Labrador.

Chapter 18. Soup!

Turn Bones and Giblets into a Winter Meal

Making soup is more what you'd call 'guidelines' than actual rules.

Soup makes the mouth happy, stomach warm, and fills a house with heavenly aroma. Scraps are transformed into delicious food. Carcass bones, necks and giblets? Floppy celery or bendy carrots past their prime? Perfect. We extend the shelf life of good produce.

By using every bit of the bird, one can show their deep respect for nature, satisfy the desire to be frugal, and eat better than a king. Making homemade soup is easy once you know how. You'll never go back to store-bought.

To make soup, you'll need to simmer water, vegetables, meat, herbs, and sometimes, a starch. Use cold water for cooking. It's not routed through a water softener.

To make Pheasant Soup, at least one carcass along with its neck and giblets is required. Depending on the contents of our freezer, we have the flexibility to change the amount of meat used. Two legs and a carcass would be hearty. So would two or even three carcasses and their necks.

Simmer the soup meat we have for two hours. Some brown froth may rise. That foam is good protein. Skim it for fancy clear soup broth, stir it back in for hearty rustic soup. Then remove all meat and bones.

Strip tender meat from carcass or bones with a fork. Not only does the neck add flavor to the broth, it also has some tasty meat. It will take some work to get it, though. Use a small serrated knife to break tough outer tissues. Pull with your fingers and chop meat into bite-sized chunks. Deboned meat goes straight back into the stockpot.

For soups like Pheasant Ramen or Pheasant Bibimbap, we would set aside the shredded pheasant meat. It's added to the guest's bowl in a decorative presentation before serving.

For hundreds of years, cooks have added sauteed onions, carrots, and celery. Leeks, too. Those flavors are a classic combination for good reason.

This recipe uses scallions to add the texture and taste of both onions and leeks in one vegetable. Chop them into eighth-inch slices, from the white base through the firm green shoots. Discard the funny little white roots and leafiest tops. Carrots and celery are washed and chopped into thick coin sized bits. I like to scrub or peel the carrots first.

Fresh green beans are a pleasant addition to the vegetable foundation. Or, replace them with a twelve ounce bag of mixed frozen vegetables (carrots, green beans, corn, peas). They are going to simmer for hours, after all. If you're short on time but still want extra flashes of color and taste, frozen veggies are a perfect solution.

The recipe calls for the pungent flavors of garlic, the earthy scent of bay leaves, the fragrant taste of thyme, and zesty notes of oregano. Lots of oregano. The final touch is a handful of freshly chopped parsley, salt, and black pepper.

Be bold, trust your tongue and judgment for the amount of spice to use, but salt and pepper added at the table add more zing. Guests can add more salt, they can't add less.

Rice, wild rice, egg noodles, ramen or pasta are all excellent additions to bulk up a soup.

Preparing the ingredients separately and combining them in bowls before serving allows for leftovers to be repurposed. We could reincarnate pheasant Rice soup as Pheasant Tortelloni soup with ease. Heat frozen broth, drop in fresh cheese tortellini for 6 minutes, serve.

Rice and wild rice are robust. You can add them to the simmering pot twenty minutes or an hour, respectively, before serving. I recommend cooking pheasant and rice soup this way.

Consider your leftovers and plan for next meals. Soup with rice freezes well. Soup with pasta can suffer from overcooking. While a fancy chef might turn up his nose at adding pasta to leftover pheasant and rice soup, I think it's a delicious gumbo.

Parting thought:

let's consider the humble Supermarket Rotisserie Chicken, hero of the working family.

If there isn't much pheasant in the freezer, the picked clean carcass, wings, skin and bones of a rotisserie chicken add meat, flavor, fat and salt. Lots of salt. Some say it's sacrilege to mix chicken and pheasant, I say it's delicious.

Simmer the raw or frozen pheasant parts available for an hour. Then add the cooked supermarket chicken remnants to the soup pot. Debone the contents an hour later. You won't believe how much meat comes off that carcass.

A complete meal only requires good fresh bread and butter.

Notes

Chapter 18.1 Recipe: Pheasant and Rice Soup

Serves: 8 Preparation: 30 minutes Cooking: 3 hours.

These are guidelines, the amounts are very general. If you only have one pheasant carcass and neck, one might reduce water by a cup or two, or increase the amount of veggies.

Ingredients:

- Uncooked pheasant carcass, neck and two legs. Or two or three carcasses/necks. Or four legs.
- 1 medium yellow onion, chopped
- 2 cups white rice.
- 1 cup scallions, chopped from white to green shoots
- 2 cups celery (about 1/3 of a bunch)
- 2 cloves garlic, minced
- 2 cups carrots, chopped into small coin sized pieces
- 2 cups green beans, ends nipped, cut into 1 inch segments
- ½ cup chopped parsley
- 2 bay leaves
- 1 Teaspoon dry thyme
- 1 Tablespoon Turkish oregano
- 1 Teaspoon fresh ground black pepper
- Salt to taste (½ Teaspoon)
- 2 teaspoons olive oil

Lets get cooking.

- ○ Brown chopped onions with olive oil in the bottom of the stock pot.

- ○ Bring pheasant parts and 10 cups cold water in covered pot to a boil. Immediately lower heat to simmer for 2 hours. Stir any brown foam or 'scum' back into the broth. Don't boil.

- ○ Use a straining ladle to remove all parts with bones to cool on a platter.

- ○ Use a fork, knife, and fingers to strip as much meat as possible from cooled bones and cartilage. Return shreds of meat to the pot. Chop heart, liver, and gizzard (if using these parts) into fine bits.

- ○ Add carrots, garlic, bay leaves, thyme and oregano. Simmer covered for 20 minutes.

- ○ Add rice, scallions, green beans and celery. Simmer for another 20 minutes.

- ○ Add parsley, pepper and salt.

Serve with a garnish of fresh ground pepper over each bowl, with good bread and butter. Enjoy!

Chapter 19: Why the Petersons Hate Coyotes

My dad took scenic drives after he retired, visiting small state parks and obscure Civil War memorials in his burnt orange Honda Element. One early November day, he discovered he was driving north. He was six hours closer to his son's family, so he kept going. Later, he phoned his wife from a rest stop, saying the car had decided to go to Wisconsin.

Back home in North Carolina, his wife, Margaret, told him to drive safe and bring home some cheese. My dad pulled into our driveway the next afternoon. His clothes were rumpled and he needed a shave.

My Labrador watched as he unpacked the back two thirds of his car. It yielded a scattered collection of long sleeve shirts, three bottles of bug spray, four tubes of sun-screen and an expensive digital camera bag that had been missing since September. We found two pair of hiking boots, two raincoats, and a cased Rossi twenty-two revolver he'd forgotten under the passenger seat. Thankfully, he'd stopped at a Walmart off the Interstate the day before, to buy underwear and socks on the trip.

I drove my Subaru the next day, claiming the dog needed his space in the back hatch. We wasted time over coffee and pastry. We lost more time jawboning at the Ace True-Value hardware store where he bought bug spray and a hunting license. It was mid-morning before our tires crunched on the gravel track in front of Roberta's house. It was a late start, but we were content.

A few red and yellow leaves still clung to the trees. The autumn air was thick with the earthy smell of the foliage that had tumbled to the ground weeks before. They lay thick in the woods. Their little dry husks piled beside the trail. We kicked them from our path and they crunched underfoot; the sunshine felt good on our backs, second-summer had arrived.

Dad had borrowed my orange vest and Ithaca shotgun, while I wore a light upland hunting jacket over jeans and a t-shirt. I carried my Beretta Ultralight with its fancy wood and engravings.

Havoc, my Labrador, was the only one serious about this hunt. He respected my dad's slow pace and unsteady gait as we walked. The dog sought the old man's approval, although they had only met the day before.

Roberta had given us permission to hunt her land, provided we shot every God-damned rabbit on sight. Those were her words. She lived on a hundred and fifty acres of old Norwegian farmstead, at the lip of a hollow protected from winter winds. The original pioneers moved to a bigger farm after they got established, their descendants were still working the big rolling farm fields around us. Berta spent her spare time reforesting a small eighty acre plot, cleared a hundred years ago. Then trouble struck.

She began her morning commute, sipping a cup of coffee in her diesel VW Jetta, then pressed the brake pedal as she approached Highway H. Her foot banged on the floorboard. No brakes. She put her travel mug in a cup holder, downshifted and used her hand brake. Then she drove to Mark's Muffler and Tire Center for a consultation.

"I dunno, Berta. If I didn't know better, I'd say someone cut your brake line." Mark pointed to a neat gash in the black rubber tube near her wheel, once her car had been raised high on the service lift.

"Fiddlesticks, dear. It's nothing but bad luck. Something sharp kicked up from the road."

The repair was not difficult or expensive, but her mechanic insisted he had never seen such a thing before.

The plot thickened as she sat at her table, eating an early Saturday breakfast. Morning rays revealed the long shadows of three ninja interlopers outside her picture window. Cottontails. Under her car, they were chewing on something. It took a moment for the pieces to fall into place.

"You little bastards!" she shouted when she burst out the back door. The rabbits scattered.

For the second time that week, cute little bunnies had attacked her car. Berta bent down to inspect the front tire and discovered a growing red puddle. She tapped a wet finger to her tongue, then spit. Sweet. Red and sweet meant brake fluid.

After the second trip to Mark's Muffler and Tire Care, she parked her car inside. There was plenty of space next to her tractor, mowing bed and bar cutter. She closed the big barn door before calling her friend Danny at the UW Extension. A few days later, he was leaning on the barbed wire fence that separated her north forty, explaining what he'd found.

"Berta, you've got a serious rabbit problem."

"I know, Danny. The little turds are trying to kill me."

"Fair point. But they're eating your saplings, too. Call every friend you've got. Get them out here, shooting rabbits." Danny showed her little brown pellets scattered liberally around every brush pile and hiding place on her property.

"I wonder how I got so many bunnies," she pondered.

It would turn out the Petersons were the cause, and it all began two years ago.

That clan, descendants of the original settlers of her land, owned all the farms surrounding her place. People referred to the three generations of menfolk, from youngest to oldest, as 'The Peterson Boys'. These big, hard working blond men were fair-minded in their dealings, and famous for their generosity, good humor, and love of a good meal.

To glorify Thanksgiving cravings, Peterson women had grown two enormous gobblers. The largest won the County Fair, cementing their reputation as domestic goddesses. The whole county knew the Peterson Thanksgiving feast was going to be special that year.

The bright white monsters waddled about their pen, with stupid expressions and garish red heads. Their succulence and flavor was anticipated with fervor, growing for weeks as the turkeys themselves grew larger. The meal was anticipated even more than deer season.

The Peterson Boys declared war and armed themselves with deer rifles. Their mission: shooting coyotes. They shot coyotes from tractors during the day, or called them with bait, and shot them in the moonlight. The righteous jihad lasted over a year until revenge seemed complete. There were no coyotes left to shoot on Peterson land.

Surrounded by Petersons, free of coyotes, Berta's bunnies bred. They ate her saplings, her berry canes, and the bark at the base of smaller trees. They chewed on her car.

Danny, from the UW-Extension, visited various Petersons. Part of his job was to find a reason for ecological imbalances. The tale of "Why the Petersons Hate Coyotes" came to light. The virtue of blasting all song-dogs to hell was extolled. Danny nodded, then put a big hank of Red Man into his cheek.

He pointed out that honor had been satisfied and wondered if they might tolerate a few coyotes. Just to keep the rabbits in check, you see.

The Peterson Boys called the vendetta off with less argument than expected. Their women had questioned the damage rabbits had done to their truck garden the previous summer, and The Boys reckoned the less discussion the better. But the bunnies still had no predators.

"It's not nice to fool Mother Nature." Dad shook his head with a smile after he heard the whole story.

I told him how The Rev, Derry and half-a-dozen braying beagles had collected a bushel basket of bunnies on this side of the Pleasant Branch creek for stew, and vowed to come back and work the other side next week. There were still plenty of rabbits, and they heard pheasants crowing at dusk.

We ambled down the slope of the dry track, through the small woods, and stepped onto a grassy overlook. The view was panoramic. Glaciers had folded that bit of earth, and runoff had done its magic. Three small valleys came together in the flat area of marsh. The trout stream winding through the hollow was icing on the cake.

"Tree rat!" My dad smiled at the scolding from a squirrel up in a tree. His pace had slowed and there was an occasional uncertainty about his bearing, but he still handled a shotgun with confidence. He'd hunted grouse and rabbits as he grew up in rural northern Pennsylvania. A tough old squirrel was not pleasing to his palate.

Havoc would return when Dad stopped, which was often. The dog checked, putting his muzzle under the old man's hand. My chest was tight, and it was hard to swallow as I watched them interact. The Labrador expressed my love and concern, without embarrassing anyone with clumsy words.

My dog was dividing his attention between hunting smells and my father, until he spotted the little bridge crossing the creek. He remembered that bridge. The pup turned his white toothy grin and pretty brown eyes towards me. After a little four-footed hop, he made a long grunt and a play-bow. He knew exactly how to turn on the cute.

"Okay. Find the water!" This was the permission he needed to light his afterburners and sprint fifty yards to the creek. Like a goofy canine lightning bolt, his back end went faster than the front. He swerved off the double-wide track, and disappeared from sight through tall grass.

My father laughed at the sight of the dog racing away. "Where is he going?"

"He loves to swim, and he'll get a drink." A short stroll later, we stood at the crown of earth mounded over a big corrugated steel drainage tube. The shaggy turf under our feet was ancient. Three feet below, a wet fox-red Labrador was grinning up. He was chest deep in clear, rippling water, lapping at it.

Our trail diverged on the other side of the bridge. One route headed up a ravine through the forest. The trunks of the trees grew through angry berry vines, sharper than barbed wire and meaner than a bear chewing bumblebees. The other path skirted the woods and followed the stream. The lower path was spotted with stands of invasive honeysuckle, brambles and Canadian thistle in thick tangles at the foot of the wooded hills.

The lower path was promising. Havoc's attention turned to the scents in the prairie grasses. Focused, his nose lowered, and his tail began to wag as a teasing scent was detected.

"I think there's a pheasant around here," I said as I drew some distance from my dad, thumb over the safety of my gun. "But it's not close, based on his tail."

Havoc swung to the other side of a low tangle of thorns he was sniffing. He was in 'detective' mode. If the scent had been stronger, he would have charged back and forth like an upland Labrador Seal-Team-Six.

"Hey!" I shouted in surprise as something struck me hard on the shin. A creature in the deep grass had struck like a torpedo, faster than I could react. "Ow!" At first, I had the silly idea I'd been bit by a python.

A harmless brown and white cottontail lay jerking and thrashing at my feet.

"What happened?" my dad called, his eyebrows raised.

Havoc wasn't interested. He backed out of the thicket, tail wagging, searching the grass behind for stronger bird scent.

"A rabbit ran into my shin and broke its neck," I replied, holding up the dead bunny.

"What?" My dad wandered closer and looked at the twitching rabbit.

The dog joined us. He nosed the bunny's body, then turned back to explore for bird scent.

"He shot through the grass, hit my shin and broke his neck." I reached down to rub my leg.

"That's the damnedest thing. Never seen that before. Anything I can do to help?"

Havoc returned to investigate whatever could possibly interest two men. He gave the dead rabbit a vigorous, insistent sniffing, and generally made a minor nuisance of himself. I didn't want my bird dog thinking rabbits were something to seek out.

"Call the dog down the path and ask him to 'find the bird'. Keep him busy while I field dress this bunny."

My father looked at me like I had asked him to talk to a toaster oven, but he gave it a try. "Havoc, can you find a bird?"

The dog snapped to attention. He ran past the old man, nose down. Dad's mouth was open as he followed.

I waved my thanks, now kneeling on the trail. I was reluctant to gut the critter. I turned my Kabar folding knife around, to hold it by the five inch blade. Then I gave the bunny a sharp whack behind its head. Convinced it was dead, I field dressed the unlucky fellow.

I wrinkled my nose against the unpleasant smell, and examined the offal for white lesions in the guts. The liver looked red and healthy. What with the overpopulation, and strange kamikaze run, I was concerned it might have tularemia, the rabbit fever.

I heard the clucking of a pheasant and boom of my father's shotgun. I jumped to my feed and wiped my bloody fingers on my trousers.

"Everything okay?" I called out, then paused to listen to the quiet countryside. No reply came. I hurried down the track, to find my father rubbing his shoulder.

"These things kick harder than I remembered," he said.

"What happened?"

"Well, that dog kicked up a pheasant. It flew to the left, across the trail, so I took a pot-shot."

"Did you hit it?"

"I probably missed by a mile. But Havoc was chasing under that bird. I hope he's not in the next county by now."

"No, he'll stay close. He's a good dog." I gave my best piercing whistle and called.

"When I was a boy, I had a beagle named Elmer Fudd. I loved that dog, but he was none too bright, always running after rabbits and getting lost." My dad was just getting warmed up, telling this story for the second time today. "I used to go across the street from my mom and dad's, after school, up into the hills. Lots of times I'd bring back a couple rabbits. That was just after the war and meat was still..."

"Hey Dad. Nice shot." I pointed to his feet.

The dog had quietly returned and lay there, a big dead cock pheasant in his mouth. A few spots of blood showed at the bird's open beak.

"Well, I'll be damned." My old man rubbed his sore shoulder and smiled. "That's a pretty good dog."

Chapter 20. Leftovers: Pheasant Salad

Sometimes luck provides more bird to cook than a family can eat in one sitting; there are leftovers to use up.

Perhaps misfortune provided a small bird, or one that is very shot up. Maybe a group of four is hoping for a meal from one bird. Here is your insanely delicious solution to these problems: Pheasant Salad.

Things to know/ why this works

What elevates this recipe above ordinary chicken salad? Each bite delights the tongue by igniting tiny flavor bombs. Salty capers, sweet chunk of apple, or a spicy bit of red onion complement a creamy foundation of soft, delicious pheasant. There is a little zing of lemon to be discovered while soft meat and crunchy celery team up. And it uses cottage cheese and mayo. I don't know why, but it works.

You can serve this sophisticated combination over the juiciest, ripe, heirloom tomato slices. It works over a bed of fresh, crunchy leafy greens. Pheasant salad is unparalleled as a sandwich served on fresh baked rolls for lunch or dinner, or over toasted bagels for breakfast.

Capers. Most people don't have capers in the 'fridge, or a clue what they are. You're shopping for tiny, expensive, salty pickled flavor grenades. Often near the pickle section of a grocery store, they are worth their price. If you see *Nonpareil* Capers or *Balsamic* capers on the shelf, those are capers. 'Nonpareil' means 'f'ing awesome' in Olde Middle English, and 'Balsamic' means 'vinegar'. Like a 'Waterproof Rain Poncho' is just a rain poncho, they're both just capers. Be aware that *caper berries* are **not** capers, neither are caperberries. Now you're an expert. (See Footnote 1)

Fine chopped red onion provides a different flavor pop and crunch. For sad people that can't tolerate red onion, substitute spicy red radish.

The pheasant breast fillet could be leftovers, cooked any way at all. Starting with an uncooked fillet, grilling with a maple/apple vinegar marinade is delicious, quick and easy. Out of season, we may substitute eight ounces of chicken or five ounces of canned tuna. If they packed the tuna in oil, eliminate olive oil from the ingredients list.

Juice, fresh squeezed from half a small lemon, is absolutely better tasting than bottled lemon juice. Even packed in a cute yellow plastic bottle and named 'real lemon', that stuff is sad. Squeeze half a small lemon—now you've got real flavor. No need to measure with a spoon, just don't choke the fruit like a ham-fisted gorilla.

I like parsley, and use more than called for. Dijon or horseradish mustard is a must, the spicier the better. Cottage cheese can be low fat or regular, small or large curd. Try to scoop more curds and less whey, but it's not critical. But mayonnaise? Please, for the love of God, don't use Miracle Whip. That's a sad excuse for the real thing.

Chop all the ingredients. Mix them completely in a mixing bowl using gentle strokes with a rubber spatula. Sprinkle and fold the dried dill last so it looks pretty.

Form the pheasant salad into a tall mound at the center. Wipe the dressing from the sides of the bowl with the spatula, for appearance. Cover with plastic wrap and refrigerate for at least thirty minutes. Gravity and refrigeration will firm up the composition, excess fluid will drain to the bottom. Every bit and drop in the bowl is delicious.

*Footnote 1- once you taste a caper, you'll be a *bona fide* expert.

Chapter 20.1 Recipe: Pheasant Salad

Serves: 4 Preparation: 12 minutes Refrigeration: 30 minutes

Cottage cheese in the Pheasant Salad dressing? Yes! This recipe will make you a believer.

Ingredients:

- One pre-cooked pheasant breast filet
- 1 teaspoon olive oil
- 1/3 cup cottage cheese
- 2 tablespoons mayonnaise
- ¼ cup red onion chopped fine
- 3 stalks celery, chopped fine
- ¼ cup apples chopped medium
- 2 tablespoons capers
- 2 teaspoons lemon juice
- 3 tablespoons fresh chopped parsley
- 1 tablespoon Dijon or horseradish mustard
- 1 large pinch of dried dill

Lets get cooking.

- o Mix all ingredients except dill completely in a mixing bowl. Then sprinkle dill and fold it into mix.

- o Form a neat towering mound in center of mixing bowl.

- o Cover and refrigerate for at least 30 minutes before serving.

Chapter 21. Leftovers: Pheasant Quiche

Real Men don't eat quiche. But they'll gobble up pheasant and bacon pie and ask for second helpings.

Things to know/ why this works

This dish is an easy choice when there are leftovers. A single pheasant breast filet, a little steamed broccoli or asparagus, and a frozen 9" deep dish pie crust are the main ingredients.

Consider doubling the recipe, since they sell pie crusts in pairs. Quiche freezes well. Thaw frozen crust, then pre-bake to cook the bottom. Raw pie dough would end up gooey if baked while creamy custard soaked from the top. No one likes a soggy bottom. Pre-baking a pie crust on the internet involves dried beans, pie crust weights, a couple bags of marbles and a pie stone. Ignore that stuff. Poke holes in the bottom of the crust with a fork. Bake at 400° F for 5 minutes. Press the dough down, it will have puffed up due to steam. Bake for another 5 minutes, then remove from the oven.

Chop pheasant and broccoli into bite size morsels, then sauté with fine chopped bacon. A little bacon packs a lot of salt and flavor.
The custard consists of four regular size eggs (or three jumbo sized) mixed with one cup of half-and-half and ground black pepper seasoning.

Cheese. You might shred some Colby, Mozzarella, and a little sharp Cheddar, or buy a package of shredded mixed cheese. Pick your favorite and the result will be delicious.

The volume of ingredients is variable and not all nine inch pie crusts carry the same volume. Pouring the custard over the solid ingredients ensures all the good stuff will fit.

Layer half the pheasant, bacon and broccoli over the bottom of the pie crust, then half the cheese. Next, the rest of the pheasant, bacon and broccoli mixture, then cover with the last of the shredded cheese. Pour custard slowly over the top, allowing it to settle deep, soaking all the ingredients below.

Sprinkle a tablespoon of freshly chopped parsley over the top, and protect the thin pie crust edge with tin foil before baking. A two inch wide strip of tinfoil, pressed around the edges, will prevent the thin edge of dough from overcooking.

If there is excess custard, fry it for a snack while the pie bakes.

Crustless Quiche.

Making crustless quiche is simple. Add an egg or two to the custard and eliminate the pie crust. Grease a pie pan (glass or metal) generously with shortening and proceed exactly as if there was a crust.

Chapter 21.1 Recipe: Pheasant Quiche.

Serves: 6 Preparation: 20-30 minutes Cooking: 1 hour.

Breakfast, lunch, or dinner—it's hard to beat pheasant quiche. Yep, bird pie!

Ingredients:

- 1 9" deep dish Pillsbury frozen pie crust (or equivalent)
- 3 slices bacon, chopped
- 1 cooked pheasant breast filet, chopped
- ¼ cup steamed broccoli, chopped coarse
- 1 cup half-and-half
- 1 cup shredded cheese.
- 4 eggs (3 jumbo sized)
- 1 tablespoon parsley, chopped
- ¼ teaspoon ground black pepper.

Lets get cooking.

- Defrost frozen pie crust. Preheat oven to 400° F.

- Prick the bottom of pie dough every 3 inches with a fork. Prebake pie crust, 5 minutes, push down dough, bake another 5 minutes, then remove from oven.

- Fry bacon, set aside and chop fine.
- Sauté cooked and chopped pheasant breast filet and broccoli in bacon grease.

- Layer pheasant, broccoli, and bacon in the pie shell with shredded cheese.

- Mix eggs, half-and-half, and ground pepper. Pour slowly over prepared fillings. Allow to settle. Sprinkle parsley on top. Protect pie crust edges with tin foil.

- Bake in the preheated oven at 400° F, until a toothpick inserted into the center comes out clean, 45 to 55 minutes. Let stand for 15 minutes before slicing.

Serve with a crisp green salad, or fresh fruit.

Gobble it down with a light bodied beer, or have it for breakfast with coffee. Try to not eat half the pie by yourself in one sitting so you'll have room for a midnight snack.

Chapter 22. A More Involved Pasta Sauce

Pasta sauce has simple ingredients. There is no trace of high-fructose corn syrup, modified soy protein, or artificial 'natural flavors'.

Keep in mind that this is cooking, not shotgun shell reloading or baking. You're expected to put more or less of each ingredient into the pot, even add new ingredients or take some out, all to your preference and taste buds. When reloading shotgun shells, follow the recipe exactly, without the smallest variation. This ain't that.

My Grandfather grew heirloom tomatoes in his backyard. Those red masterpieces got more attention, and care than most of his 52 grandchildren. My Grandmother grew her own fresh herbs: oregano, basil, parsley, and cilantro. Combined, she used these ingredients to make Zen Level Five pasta sauce. Unparalleled. Which brings us to the quality of your ingredients.

In this complicated, modern world, we balance convenience, cost, and excellence. The best dried spices are fresh from a specialty shop. Dried herbs are more powerful than when fresh, but they lose flavor over time. Best quality is your best buy. Oregano, basil, parsley, rosemary, thyme, and fennel are all more powerful when dried. Except for dried parsley, which is useless. Fortunately, parsley is easy to get fresh.

Garlic should always be fresh. Pull a few cloves from the head, peel and crush them with the flat of a kitchen knife blade, use a fancy garlic press, or smack them with a mallet, like my Mom.

Onion will be chopped into quarter-inch chunks, cooked in hot oil until clear with brown edges, not thrown away like in our easy recipe.

Canned, crushed tomatoes and tomato paste are used. These ingredients are usually salted. Seasonal ripe heirloom tomatoes would be the very best, but are an impractical inconvenience for most home cooks.

Notes

Chapter 22.1 Recipe: A More Involved Pasta Sauce.

Serves 8 to 10 Preparation: 10 minutes Cooking: 1 hour 30 minutes.

When cooking for two, it's hard to beat sauce from a jar. But for larger gatherings or if you just want to make the point that you can do better—here's a recipe for you to start modifying!

Ingredients:

- ½ medium yellow onion, diced
- 1 28 ounce can tomato puree
- 1 6 ounce can tomato paste
- 2 tablespoons olive oil
- 3 cloves garlic
- 2 tablespoons dried basil
- 1or 2 tablespoons dried oregano
- 1 teaspoon salt
- 1-2 teaspoons sugar
- ½ teaspoon ground black pepper.

Lets get cooking.

- o Brown onions in 6 quart stock pot with 2 tablespoons olive oil. This will take about 5 minutes once the pot comes to medium-high heat.

- o Stir and scrape with wooden spoon.

- o Lower heat. Add tomato puree, tomato paste, and garlic. Simmer for 1 hour.

- o Add oregano, basil, salt, sugar and pepper. Simmer another 30 minutes.

That's your big pot of pasta sauce, as good as any you'll find.

With a little practice and experimenting, perfect this recipe to your tastebuds. Soon, you'll be throwing spices into the pot by the palmful or pinch. With a sip of sauce from your wooden spoon, you might mutter, "Ah! But it needs more..."

Chapter 23. Ricky and the Model 37.

"I want to play with my trucks." Kneeling on the faded tan carpet, Ricky ignored his grandmother. He pushed a toy dump truck around a pile of blocks beside a small backhoe. They made toys of sturdy painted sheet metal back in those days.

"Don't you sass me like that. It's time for your nap." Thin and gray haired, the woman's voice pitched higher and cracked. Her elbows hugged to her sides, thin frail hands lined with blue veins began to shake. She wore a blue floral house dress under a white full apron. Clear cat-eye glasses hung about her neck from a silver chain. "You used to be good. Your sister needs her nap, too."

The little boy looked up, then jumped to his feet. He took her thin hand in his plump grip. "Sorry Grandma." His gaze flickered through the open parlor door. Kathy, his younger sister, was sound asleep, sprawled on the folding cot inside.

Grandma led him through the small dining room, then prompted him up steep narrow pine stairs with a ribbed black rubber runner. Old brown linoleum covered the dark second floor landing. The black pot-belly oil burner hid in the gloom, but it's faint yellow pilot light drew Ricky's attention, as it always did. They turned and entered a bright clean bedroom.

Clear pine wainscoting covered three walls, bookshelves behind spotless glass doors covered the other. The room was filled with a small desk, dresser, gun cabinet and single bed. Subtle waves and wrinkles in the glass windows were framed with blue draperies. These looked out on an empty lot and three small houses before a steel bridge that crossed the Allegheny river. The boy could see the neighborhood baseball field in the distance below towering green hills.

Grandma pulled the drapes closed, then set the broad dial of a squat white Lux timer with a rattling twist. "Thirty minutes." The kitchen timer ticked its little metronome beat as she pulled the door halfway closed. Ricky heard the stairs creak as she retreated.

He flopped onto the bed, restless. Nap time was boring. He rolled over to look through the glass doors at his father's old mitt and a baseball with signatures and a trophy cup. There were paperback books with rocket ships and spacemen on the cover, and big books full of long hard words he couldn't read. His father said they were about HAM radio. *Impedance, rectifier, variable-frequency oscillator.* They had sounded these words out together, but the books remained a mystery.

Ricky rolled to his other side, restless. His eyes lingered on the rifles. Eight long guns on display with a small hutch below. He had stern direction to never touch these. The magnificent guns shined with deep blue metal and polished wood. With a glance at the half-open bedroom door, he crept to put his finger on the lever of the most attractive. He inhaled, filling sinuses with the scent of Hoppe's Number Nine Gun Bore Cleaner. It was sweet and persistent deep in his nose; a scent that would stay with him forever.

He twisted the sleek rifle on its butt to admire the lines of its stock. He knew it was a Savage 99. Father told him all the gun names, while oiling each on a layer of newspaper over the dresser last night. The tiny old bolt action Savage four-ten was a sad pipsqueak in comparison, but Dad said he could use it. They would go shooting, and the boys' gun was for him. It leaned in the corner of the gun rack, too short to reach the felt-lined crosspiece.

His mother was not happy about the plan. Dad told her that boys learned to shoot at the quarry when they were six years old, and it was time to get him a baseball mitt, too. Mom didn't like guns. Grandma clucked. Disapproval made the chance to shoot even more exciting.

Turning a bigger gun sideways, the engravings transfixed him. He had noticed these pictures the night before. A hunting dog pointed at two strange long birds. The scene was in a field surrounded by hills. The other side of the gun had ducks, which he disregarded. With a calculated glance at the bedroom door, he lifted the big shotgun from its resting place, then laid it across the bed-covers.

Placed sideways on the bed, he absorbed the panoramic image etched deep in shiny metal. Alone in the room, he had time to study the scene capturing a dog's fascination. Those were pheasants, Dad said, but this was grouse country. Mom had said "no dogs."

Ricky set the big gun back in the rack. He wanted a big dog.

Sitting cross-legged on the carpet, he opened the small under-cabinet and removed a long metal box without making a sound. Opening the dark green lid, he touched thin metal shafts and thick wooden rods, threaded at the ends. White linen patches, bronze brushes, and metal loops on threaded fittings filled small compartments. He set the cleaning kit aside.

Flat Remington boxes held wicked looking cartridges capped with shiny copper bullets. They were dull gray at the tip, smooth, and perfectly made. The boxes were heavy for their size. Ricky organized these on the carpet beside him.

Heavy square paper cartons had 'Peters' printed on top in big block letters. Inside were fat green, smooth paper tubes with clever star-shaped folds at one end and brass at the other. Shotgun shells. Their sharp tangy scent was powerful, yet good. One carton held skinny shells with green ribbed sides.

Puny yellowed Winchester boxes sported a cowboy on horseback, galloping hell for leather. These held his interest; he examined the tiny twenty-two caliber bullets within.

Curiosity satisfied, he returned the ammunition neatly to their cubby, just as he had found them. He crept back to the bed, curled up, and listened to the ticking of the kitchen timer. His eyes closed, time passed, he fell asleep.

Fifty years later, he had a young bird dog and an Ithaca Model 37 of his own. Dad had sold the 16 gauge when it got hard to find ammunition, but this twelve gauge '37 seemed to complete the circle.

Chapter 24. Buying the Right Shotgun

"I would rather hunt pheasants with a good dog and a sack of rocks than go without the dog. Any shotgun that goes 'boom!' is better than a sack of rocks." - Me.

Here are some guidelines to consider:

The best shotgun is one that fits. Stock fitting is a matter of arm length, shoulder width, neck length, cheek placement, hand size, and flexibility. They are bent for right or left-handed shooters. A sub-group of sportsmen will find that a straight stock is the best cast for them. There are smaller youth shotguns, and shotguns designed for the anatomy of the average woman. These are starting points. Birds are safe when a shotgun doesn't fit.

Weight is important. An upland shotgun should be six to seven pounds. This is a 'walk much, shoot little' sport. Success will hinge on a few good shots. Over seven pounds is a chore to carry, especially after the third mile of a hike. But a five pound gun has brutal recoil. Good fit and heavy guns mitigate recoil. It's a trade-off.

You can't go wrong with a 12 gauge. Ammunition is common and less expensive. It's easy to find shells that cover the entire range of games and quarry. Twelve gauges do not kick harder than a twenty, because recoil depends on the shells, not the size of the muzzle.

Europe, California, and some parts of South Dakota presently mandate non-toxic shot for upland hunting. Non-toxic shot requirements will continue to expand. The larger twelve gauge shells future-proof your shotgun. The extra room in a 12 gauge shell is an advantage for the bulkier steel or bismuth payloads in non-toxic shot shells.

A twenty gauge may fit short hunters better. Twenties often weigh less, and size smaller than a twelve. But they can deliver the same stout 1 ¼ ounce 1330 fps lead payload. Ammunition will be more difficult to find and cost more. For rabbits, grouse, quail or partridge, 20 gauge offers more choices for the smaller payloads appropriate for these game animals. Twenty gauge is at a disadvantage when using non-toxic shot because of their smaller shells.

Used is good. Some new shotguns will not survive the first box of shells. Most failures occur in the first two hundred rounds while a good used shotgun will last a hundred years. The right used shotgun is by far your smartest purchase. A reputable specialty gun shop or a knowledgeable friend from your gun club can help navigate these waters.

Spend enough for quality. There are many mid-range guns a hunter would be proud to own for a lifetime. Some cheap shotguns will give one hunter excellent service. Another with the same make and model will experience nothing but frustration. With a cheap shotgun, you're the quality control department. Don't be a cheapskate. A decent shotgun might cost between a week or two of your paycheck, before deductions.

The best inexpensive double-barrel shotgun is a semi-automatic. Economical and reliable, semi-autos are a better value than cheap two-barrel shotguns. Semi-automatics are the simplest mechanical design other than the single-shot single-barrel shotgun. The single shot is a solid workhorse, but you'll often appreciate a second or third shot.

Pump shotguns are hard to beat for price and reliability. A used 12 gauge Ithaca Model 37 or Remington Wingmaster make fine choices. Fixed choke, in modified or full constriction, is not a disadvantage for the pheasant hunter. If a fellow also hunts grouse and turkey, screw-in chokes or the old-fashioned Polychoke are desirable. If you spot a Polychoke on an old gun, you can see how ugly they are. But they really work.

If you must have two barrels, pay the proper price of admission. You can't go wrong with a used Browning Citori or Beretta 686. Well-to-do hunters with multiple shotguns can afford to experiment with cheap firearms. For those with only one gun, mechanical failure ends the hunting season. It won't be fixed in time, even if the shotgun has a warranty. The hunter on a budget can't afford to buy replacements.

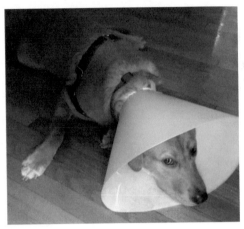

Warranty. A lifetime warranty lasts only as long as the outfit promising to honor it. Some importers provide excellent service, while some provide months of excuse. Importers go out of business every few years, others have been around for a century.

The author expresses a fondness for many (but not all) shotguns from Beretta, Browning, and Ceasar Guirini/Fabarms/Syren as well as Ithaca Model 37 and Remington Wingmaster.

As always, Caveat Emptor. Let the buyer beware.

About the Author

My name is Richard Moran. I retired as a teacher and scientist about five years ago and now spend my free time in the autumn hunting pheasants in South Central Wisconsin.

I hope you've read this book, enjoyed it, and are ready to become the expert. Make something delicious for dinner. If your partner puts up with half the nonsense mine does, they deserve it.

Made in the USA
Thornton, CO
12/06/24 09:50:09

f4ae15e4-f22c-4729-8fc8-3250858857f8R01